RAPED!!! "PRESUMED INNOCENCE"

My Fifty-Yearlong Painful Secret

DAWN MAREE KETTERINGHAM, B.A., M.A.Ed.

A very true short story which has taken a lifetime to write.

Copyright© 2015

Except as provided by the Copyright Act (rev. 2012),

NO PART of this publication may be reproduced,

stored in a retrieval system or transmitted

in any form, or by any means, without the

prior written permission of

Dawn Maree Ketteringham, B.A., M.A.Ed.,

Mary Lee MacDonald,

MEMORIES to MEMOIRS PUBLISHING and

PARAGON ECLECTIC EDITING

First Edition

All rights reserved.

ISBN: 978-0-9920417-0-0

Disclaimer

Identifying names have been changed to initials

or omitted wherever appropriate.

Dedications and Acknowledgements

I would like to dedicate this novel to my children, Brandon, (spouse, Lisa), and Drew (spouse, Jeremy), and my grandchildren, Troy, Kaylierain and Daylan, all of whom have both made me crazy, and kept me sane! I also thank my beautiful birth "mother", Berneice Ketteringham who gave me life and guides my every step from Heaven. Though we only spent the first six weeks of my life together, I have come to understand she suffered a lifetime of grief over losing me, and without her sacrifices, heartaches and unfaltering love, hope and courage, I know that my exceptional little family would not even exist. Equally I give my thanks to my wonderful adoptive Daddy, William Alexander Stewart MacDonald, Esq., who sustained my life with unconditional and unending love and whom I have never ceased to adore. My Daddy guided my path daily and taught me I could "do anything I set my mind to do". His biggest dream was to see me attend University. Though he went to Heaven just three months after I started my first semester at the University of Guelph, his steadfast encouragement and confidence in me provided the impetus for me to eventually fulfill his dream, in spades. Thanks, also, to my other 'sister', Renate, (Reni), McDonald, for life-long love, support and encouragement and to my good friends the Reverends Joan and Peter Gericke, for incessant, uplifting love and prayers. I thank my wonderful brother, Edward George (aka. Richard Ketteringham) whose 25-year search for me culminated in the rescue of myself and my children, and the clever engineering of our refuge in the safety of my home country, Canada.

Thanks to all for guiding me to be the daughter, woman, mother, grandmother, sister, friend and author that I am today. Naturally, my sincerest apologies if I have overlooked acknowledging anyone.

Dawn Maree Ketteringham B.A., M.A.Ed.,
[Aka. Mary Lee MacDonald, (Simpson),
Nee: Dawn (Ketteringham) Faulconer]

Inspirations

There is no greater agony than bearing an untold story inside you.
Dr. Maya Angelou [3]

We gain strength, and courage, and confidence by each experience in which we really stop to look fear in the face ... we must do that which we think we cannot.
Eleanor Roosevelt [1]

If you become aware of a lie and you do nothing to expose the lie, then you become part of the lie.

Dave von Kleist [2]

The circumstances of a person's life may create around them an invisible, protective outer shell to help each individual cope. However, it can never form too impervious a surface that a tiny seed of hope cannot penetrate even a sliver of a crack, and burst through with the exquisiteness of a life, well-deserved and worthy of living, blossoming, beautifying and regenerating.

Dawn Maree Ketteringham, 2013

Table of Contents

    Preface

    Introduction ………………………………………………………………………1

    Chapter 1: The Dirty Deed ……………………………………………………3

    Chapter 2: Am I Back? ………………………………………………………..5

    Chapter 3: The Gorilla …………………………………………………………7

    Chapter 4: Who Was that Great Ape? ……………………………………10

    Chapter 5: Tattered, Shattered and Scattered Pieces …………………12

    Chapter 6: What the Hell!!?? ………………………………………………15

    Chapter 7: No, *I'm* So Sorry ………………………………………………18

    Chapter 8: I've Gotta Git Outta this Place ………………………………22

    Chapter 9: My Great Escape ………………………………………………25

    Chapter 10: No Place to Run ………………………………………………27

    Chapter 11: A Place to Hide ………………………………………………30

    Chapter 12: I Still Have to Go Home ……………………………………33

    Chapter 13: "L." Needs Me …………………………………………………34

    Chapter 14: I'm On My Way ………………………………………………37

    Chapter 15: Testosterone Netherworld …………………………………40

    Chapter 16: Come Up and See His Etchings! …………………………45

Chapter 17: The Set-Up 49

Chapter 18: "MONSTER"! 53

Chapter 19: Rulers, Yardsticks and Other Torturous Implements! 58

Chapter 20: **Ahhhhhhhhhhhhhhhhhhhhhhhhhhhhhhh!!!!!!!!!!** 65

Chapter 21: Wiser eyes: Removing the Rose Tints 67

Chapter 22: "…never tried this before!" 68

Chapter 23: Forgiveness 71

Chapter 24: Disclosing My Secret 74

Chapter 25: Never Just Once! 81

Chapter 26: Letter to J.S. 83

Chapter 27: The Vicious Cycle 85

Chapter 28: And the Beat Goes On… 88

Appendix "A" 89

Epilogue 90

References 91

About the Author 94

Preface

To the best of my recollection this is my completely true memory of, and reflections about, my having been deceived, lured, entrapped, held against my will and forcibly raped, as a naïve, innocent, fourteen-year-old virgin child.

The details of my story have been haunting my thoughts and fuelling my emotional roller-coaster for over fifty years. What I describe herein are the particulars of my life story which have until now, produced a blockage forming a "creativity bottleneck". This has been hindering me from proceeding with several other manuscripts which have remained in varying stages of completion. I found it necessary to pluck these memories from my mind and "clear the slate" before continuing my writings.

I apologize in advance for the "graphic" nature of my story, however, "It is what it is." And this is my story exposing the **truth** of my personal experiences, no matter how painful, and embarrassing it has been for me to confront and accept these truths. In order to reveal and share my details within the confines of this novel, from the depths of my psyche I have had to dredge up a great courage that I never knew existed within me. I believe Dr. Maya Angelou best expressed this process for me when she wrote,

"There is something which impels us to show our inner souls.

*The more courageous we are, the more we succeed in **explaining what we know**."* [3]

With the greatest **courage**, "explaining what [I] know" is exactly what I have tried to accomplish. And, I believe that by sharing my experience through this *autobiographical novel, I will finally set my soul free from my personal agony's bondage. I can only hope for such catharsis. In the very least, it is my sincerest desire that my shared story will help another victim come to terms with the painful memories of her, or his, own experience of childhood abuse, molestation, torture and/or rape.*

Introduction: I Have Surely Died, Haven't I?

Spastic shudders pulsed and convulsed through my naked innocence. I was only a little girl — my "Daddy's little girl", a naïve and inexperienced "child" and very over-protected by my adoptive parents. That *day* was only a few months after my fourteenth birthday which I had celebrated with my two best girlfriends, by taking in the matinee movie, "Beach Party" [4], starring "Frankie and Annette". That's Frankie Avalon and Annette Funicello [5], who were popular teen actors appearing much larger than life on that gargantuan movie screen! On a sunny, sandy California beach they were doing what they do best — dancing and bopping around amongst many other bikini-clad teens. That's when I was an *innocent*, with no knowledge of any of the carnal activities experienced between men and women, let alone between teenage boys and girls. Least of all I had no concept of "rape" — and how a man could possibly perpetrate such a criminal felony — an act of violent, forced intercourse, especially on an unwilling and terrified young girl, such as myself. However after my shocking introduction to rape — I was *innocent* no longer.

What a terribly devastating turn my simple, little, insignificant life had taken on that frighteningly fateful day. The sun's glowing, golden radiance, sweet breezes and cloud-dotted azure skies, though omnipresent, omniscient overseers of my little world, were merely silent, distant witnesses of the precious jewels purloined of my ravaged innocence.

Was I still alive? Hadn't I died? Recognizing how much I desperately needed to die, I couldn't believe I was still suffering existence on this earthly plane. So, maybe I should just kill myself — but how!!??

Suddenly, my thoughts refocussed as I recognized an irrepressible trembling emanating from depths of the Mariana's trench of my withering soul's ocean. It was just barely enough of a vibration to indicate to me that, unfortunately, there was still some semblance of existence, perhaps not actual *life*, and certainly no *light*, but the shadow of a bare, struggling, stifled *existence* still remaining within me.

Chapter 1: The Dirty Deed

As I felt the warm, wet, sticky reminder oozing from inside of me and dripping down my inner thighs, an overwhelming terror immobilized my body. The strangely unfamiliar milky-white liquid had come from *his* body — from *his* penis at the summit of his seemingly elated release, and obviously propelled by some form of either delight, or malevolence, though which, I certainly could not distinguish. This ejaculate filled the previously sealed, virginal vaginal cavity of my pure, milky-white young body. Even more of the thick, mucous-like substance clung to the soft, pale skin between my innocent breasts.

My mind was numb with shock. I couldn't think or speak, or hardly even *see* as I tried to face the horrible reality of what had just happened to me — of what *I* had just been forced to *endure*. Standing up, I fearfully lowered my gaze to evaluate my battered body. Staring in outrageous disbelief, I witnessed the bloody rivers flowing from my innocence-broken, winding around and painting narrow brushstrokes on my slender inner thighs. From his repeatedly violent thrusts I could determine that the bruising had already begun to appear on the soft flesh of my tender inner thighs.

Stinging tears clouded my eyes as I visually traced the bloody stream across the baby-blue-innocence of carpet, from where I stood, back to those revealing crimson-splattered sheets. Although once stark-white, those linens were now only reminiscent, and no longer representative, of my protected, and apparently, much *coveted*, youthful virginity.

Even though I actually stood alone in the room, I could still sense his lumbering presence, as if he were still lying on top of me. This violent coward used his huge, ugly penis to rip wide-open this sealed orifice of my diminutive body — a body which now throbbed with the agony of my plundered purity. What escaped from inside of me were my youthful naïveté, my trusting nature, my beliefs in the innate goodness of others ... and absolutely all of my eternally hopeful, little girl "princess" dreams. In essence, my life, as I knew it, abruptly ended. All of these aspects of me were bursting from a strangely unfamiliar internal pressure, in the same manner that steam squeals from a rumbling kettle at full-boil.

Excruciating stabs of pain felt as if shards of broken glass had split-apart my untouched young vagina, continuing to rape me repeatedly, in tandem with each beat of my heart. My wrists were inflamed, burning from the single-handed, wrapping grasp of his massive calloused paw. My lips had been rubbed red-raw and I gagged repeatedly from the reminder of his slobbering mouth stealing and suffocating the breath from mine.

Suddenly my stomach began to rise up into the back of my throat which responded by undulating in an attempt to expel the thick, slimy, peppery after-taste of his nasty *cum*. The semen in my throat had been the direct result of my rapist's delightful, vigorous and unexpected ramming his nasty, reeking, huge cock deeply into my small throat. When I stretched open my mouth to scream, only a silent, stifled, primal cry of anger cowered in the depths of my throat, choking and gagging me *yet again*!

I wanted — no desperately *needed* to disappear, or hit this man, or rip him apart, or stab this horrible Neanderthal. Instead, I would just quietly slip away and hide my secret in clandestine shadows for the next fifty-one years!

Chapter 2: Am I Back?

As suddenly and shockingly as a soul must return from and out-of-body experience, it seemed as if my being's inner light had been sucked back-in from the clandestine shadows of its temporary emotional imprisonment. Momentarily, from this cowardly animal's grasp, my thoughts had been far removed a remote distance from the twisted, snaking veils of time and space. But this pseudo-conscious state in which my mind was drowning, suddenly switched to pin-point sharp awareness.

By focusing and listening intently, I interpreted the background noise, ascending from the downstairs rec-room, as the raucous laughter of several of the young men. Yet, I still could not hear the anticipated distinctive giggling of any *girls*. So, where were the girls? The men's voices floated on the ghostly, smoky trails, winding curiously and ascending from the basement game room. Though I couldn't distinguish the exact words, nor the precise tone of the conversations, the muffled sounds and distinctive smells created the sensation within me that the walls were deliberately squeezing me, pushing in on me and further smothering my innocence. Still, the assaulting laughter rumbled and rose up from the rec-room. Every sound and smell was overwhelming my senses. Everything seemed to be steamrolling nearer and nearer and sounding progressively louder — and LOUDER!

Slowly becoming cognizant of the *lethal* possibilities of my predicament, I was terrorized by the thought that *he* would return — this time to certainly finish the job he started and *surely kill me*. Yet my senses continued to notify me that he had never really *left* my presence. With revulsion, I sensed his face imprinting onto my face; even his breath had become my breath. In vain I tried to stop thinking about the smell and taste of his heavy, sour breath. Of course it was not only his inept oral hygiene causing his appalling breath; but it was also revoltingly soured by the regurgitated "Molson's" [7], Something-or-Other beer. I had never even tasted alcohol before being raped by this man, but for these many decades to follow, I have choked at even the slightest smell of that, or any other *beer* — a stench *forever* indelibly carved onto my brain.

Chapter 3: The Gorilla

Because J.S.'s groping gorilla hands were so enormous, he had easily grabbed both my wrists with one hand and stretched my arms up high over my head, sort of stringing me up by my wrists, as it were. He never released this one-handed vice grip, not even when he dragged me across the small room and threw me backwards onto the crumpled sheets on S.'s unmade bed. This Monster quickly muffled my protests with his mouth and his nasty, thick tongue, and he never eased the robotic clamp which his gorilla-like hand molded around both my diminutive, child-sized wrists.

All I could think of was, *what would stop him from killing me?* Since no one came to my rescue when I yelled at the outset of this violent, felonious attack, I was certainly too terror-stricken to holler for help in the aftermath. So I swallowed my screams, convinced that any appeals at that point, might draw *unwanted attention* from my rapist or his so-called *friends* — his football cronies down in the rec-room. Instinctively I knew that such attention could possibly turn this singular violation into the incomprehensible — a gang rape, which may or may not have been the original intention of the rest of his fellow "team" members downstairs. At that point, I just had no way of knowing for certain what their collective intentions could possibly be. Summarily I disallowed myself the agony of contemplating such a nightmare. Dwelling on such deranged possibilities would send my thoughts careening so far over the edge of the fiery, volcanic pit of my fear, I may never be able to reel my mind safely back to sanity.

Prohibiting such dark thoughts, I cocooned myself tightly with the once, stark-white top sheet which had met an early demise as a bloodied, crumpled, spent pile on the end of S.'s bed. Both of the new Percales [8], had been unobtrusive observers of the violence delightfully inflicted by J.S. I began to focus, to concentrate — actually to *obsess* over the irony and poetic injustice that such lovely linens, once so starched, so pure, so tightly interwoven, had now been morphed into permanently disfigured candy-caned witnesses now undoubtedly destined for swift and sure elimination.

My body ached, my heart ached more, but my soul, my pure young spirit, ached the most. Suddenly I felt as if I had been rolling and wallowing in piles of reeking excrement — in shit —

dog shit, cow shit, sheep shit — whatever! My being was now condemned to filthy, nasty contamination! It was the way I imagined a whore — no even worse — a *leper* would certainly feel. I was convinced that once word of my rape dashed around the hallowed halls of L. High School, it would doom me to be societally cast out, far from the *real* human beings, denigrated, defiled and defamed from this moment of dark destiny, until forever.

My entire existence changed in the instant of my private violation. How in the world could I ever go out in public, or to church, or the library, or swimming, or absolutely anywhere? I felt deeply ashamed and guilty as if I had done something so terribly wrong in my life that I would deserve such unspeakable punishing karma to be meted upon *me*. My mind flashed with thoughts of my future. How, someday, would I ever know if a boy really loved me, or if he'd only verbalized such words because he'd heard I was "easy", that I "put-out", that I was "sleazy" – or even worse, that I had earned the dreaded reputation as a "dirty slut"?

I wondered again, how J.S. could hurt me so badly, while several presumably "honourable" young men in the game room downstairs, just a few steps away, actually only a couple feet below the floor of S.'s bedroom. Could not one of those cowardly "jocks" or "wannabees" acknowledge my cries, or my muffled screams as J.S. was delighting in ripping me apart from the inside out? Why didn't they come up the stairs and stop him, or help me at all? Were they all so seriously fearful of falling from his god-like favour? Granted, they never responded to my protestations *prior* to the instant of my attack, but why were they ignoring my attempts at screaming for help, *during* my fierce rape? Why? I had never experienced such a feeling of isolation, abandonment and utter helplessness.

As if these thoughts weren't overwhelming enough, the worst one repeatedly pierced my brain with further undulating waves of shock. Was it possible these guys were actually a *part of* this whole horrific scenario? Perhaps each imagined he was next to partake of what they must seemingly have perceived as my coveted innocence. Which of the other "men" downstairs, the rest of the football jocks who were drinking beer and laughing uproariously, were expecting to take their turns at raping me? Oh my God!! I was suddenly keenly aware of my need to escape that room, that house, invisibly of course so as not to be caught and further victimized.

Just then, the laughter reached a crescendo which was so much louder than before, I was absolutely convinced that they were laughing **about me**! After all, **he** had **laughed at me**, hadn't he?! It was immediately after he had released his anger-filled *load* and climbed off me. He stood up like a great towering, hulking, sweating, brown behemoth and he loudly bellowed the words which my broken heart will no doubt carry throughout all of my eternal incarnations and beyond. His heartless words were certainly audible enough for all of the guys downstairs to hear when he made his grand, bedside announcement, "**HAHAHAHAHA!** So you **WERE A VIRGIN!** I guess 'Sticks' lied. But, don't you even **think** about telling anybody about this, because **I'll KILL YOU and YOUR WHOLE FAMILY!**"

Of course I believed him. And I began feeling so diminutive as my once-vibrant soul further retreated into its own, newly tailored nanospheric shell.

"AAAAAAAAAAAAHHHHHHHHHHHHHHHHHH!!!!!!!!!!!!!!!!!!!!!!"

That was the sound of my soul screaming at such an *astute* and callous observation from my rapist! I wondered why he felt it necessary to comment on my virginity immediately *after* he ripped it from its moorings behind my pristine hymen and *stole* it from me, forever. He was still laughing as he left the room, and increasingly I felt as if I were a damaged doll. I certainly did not feel like a diminutive, innocent and flesh-and-blood child—just a frail little girl.

Chapter 4: Who Was This Great Ape?

J.S. was such a *huge* man, muscular and bulky in stature, standing head-and-shoulders above all the others, even towering over the tallest boys in the last row, in his eleventh grade class photo. With his shirt off, I could not help but notice that the caramelized body smothering mine, was deeply intoxicated with an over-abundance of sunlight. Misdirected anger actually seemed to burn right through his glistening, fiery skin. I have no idea how some girls may have regarded his face as handsome, if in fact any actually did. I could see nothing beyond an icy viciousness emanating from his eyes which darkened as his evil intentions were swiftly manifested through his malevolent actions.

Obviously his size was both the reason for, and the result of, his football *frolics*. I felt certain after my terrifying victimization that he had to be at least eight or nine feet tall, and I had no doubt he had to weigh no less than six- or-seven-hundred pounds. Oh God! Why couldn't I have just died under this hippo's suffocating weight? (I suppose it would be worthy to mention that, not surprisingly his "manhood" was sized correspondingly, thus making his instrument of rape that much more threatening and violating to my young, unbroken and previously untouched hymen.)

Why was this virtual stranger even remotely interested in my thin, young, inexperienced, virginal body? I was absolutely baffled by this question. I was only a newbie, a frosh, a freshman, just starting the ninth grade. This yeti had, to my knowledge, never so much as glanced in my direction. Why would he do such a thing to me? J.S. was the proverbial jock-on-the-pedestal, supposedly the top athlete and in 1964, when he perpetrated this felony. He played Junior Football at L. High School in Toronto. I believe, in the very least he held the coveted title of "Quarterback", or possibly he was the team "Captain". I really didn't know since I had never had even the most infinitesimal interest in the sport of football, or the players — especially him!

Of course, he was very popular with the girls, or more specifically, "his girls", the *cheerleaders* and "wannabee-cheerleaders". Nevertheless, all the girl-groupies would part the aisles whenever his *real* girlfriend showed up. After all, it was common knowledge that he was dating, or possibly even engaged to, the "Barbie Doll" [7], of our school. Beautiful and popular, talented and smart, she, (who shall herein remain nameless to protect *her* innocence), seemed to be the "Prez-of-Everything" in our school, and certainly, from all appearances and *unlike me*, no doubt rich as well. Ha—it would be a sure bet to say that J.S.'s giant cock never torpedoed its way into any orifices of *her* body, at least not by force and possibly not at all. (She certainly *carried* herself as if she were a *sterile, sealed* virgin).

This fraudulent excuse for a man even had his own little trailing of guy-groupies who stuck to him like white-on-rice, or from my perspective, more appropriately in his case, like flies on shit! Strangely enough though, he actually seemed to prefer the company of those guys, those "wannabee-jocks" who were just wimpy followers. It was probably because they worshipped and idolized him as if he were a god, and if they were lucky, he would grace them with his towering presence or at least permit them to glom onto his shadow! Of course the remainder of his entourage were the real jocks — his team members — his drinking pals — his *yes-men* who were continually kowtowing to his every whim! As far as I was concerned they were all basically apprentice "Assholes" in the making!

Nevertheless, quite unbelievably everyone seemed to have a high opinion of this snake, which *I* discovered was certainly unwarranted. Apparently, J.S. was considered an all-around-great-guy, but that was undoubtedly, most especially in his *own* mind and through his *own* self-aggrandizing propaganda. It was indisputable that he was an eleventh grader at the time; however, I would later wonder from what I witnessed of his *obvious* lack of intellect, if he hadn't failed a grade at least once or twice. Furthermore, if I had to guess, I'd diagnose his verbal ineptitude as a direct result of too many drop-kicks to his head!

Chapter 5: Tattered, Shattered and Scattered Pieces

All my soul's innocent dreams of my future had, at the instant of my rape, exploded and fragmented, shattering like the slivered shards of a luckless fractured mirror. I had to *do* something — but what? A shiver rippled over my skin as some level of conscious awareness was gradually increasing inside my spirit. I could detect by the hoots and hollers I was hearing, that my rapist had in fact, descended to the testosterone-fueled, machismo nether regions, otherwise known as the "rec-room". Of course I had no idea how long I'd be able to remain *alone* in that small bedroom. After all, they *were* all males, they all had dicks and I couldn't know who would be next in line for purpose-driven penetration *of me*. I quickly realized I had to somehow pull myself together and apply my convincing and comfortable *facade of innocence*. It was a posture to which I knew I could always resort. It had succeeded in serving me well in bluffing and hiding the *many dark secrets* which comprised this petite, uninitiated little girl's weighty thirteen-year emotional baggage.

I had to somehow escape to the shadowy, unknown possibilities crowding my thoughts — and *run* home. "Run" — what was I thinking? "Home" — Oh my God, how could I possibly go home considering the broken emotional, and battered physical, state in which I was frozen? I could not even entertain the thought of facing my elderly, adoptive parents who would certainly be out in the yard doing their usual Saturday gardening. How could they possibly fathom what had just happened to me? Certainly I knew I could *never, ever* tell my frail and ailing Daddy, whose heart was already too weak for even the simplest of disappointments. Knowledge of this horrendous violation of his "innocent little girl" would surely kill him — that much I knew for certain! I couldn't live with myself if discovery of my rape brought harm to him. I certainly didn't have the right to kill this man who was undisputedly one of God's own angels caught in time, somewhere between this earthly plane and the Heavenly realms to which he truly belonged.

Yet, oh my God how desperately I wanted to tell my Daddy, my "*bestest*" friend in the whole wide world. I needed to share my pain and my fears and unload the burden of what a terrible battering my fragile little body had just withstood from this criminal assault. Desperately I craved to just be held tightly and told, "Everything is going to be alright, Little Bunny." However, in fact everything was never going to be alright again — never, and I had no idea then exactly how long "never" would be! In any event, I decided that my fragile Daddy's health and life were of exceedingly greater importance to me than my own life, or my need of his gentle comforting. At that life-changing instant, I knew that my Daddy should, and would, *never* know of this brutal rape and violation of his innocent, "Darling Little Bunny".

I already knew that my so-called "Mother" would never care one miniscule iota about my fears, my devastation or my emotional or physical pain. Instead, this hateful woman could be counted on to react in her usual vicious manner and actually delight in exploiting such terribly bad news to hurt my Daddy. Telling her would be a huge mistake—*huge*! So I vowed that neither she, nor my precious Daddy could ever know about my rape. And I never told either of them, at least not while Daddy's feet and mine shared tandem steps across this plane's same fields. I determined that immediately after the fact, and forever, hiding my dark, shameful secret, would require some serious posturing. Of course, after I cleaned myself up, I knew I would have to appear somewhat *normal* — at least on the outside.

I had to quickly assess my damage and formulate some sort of plan. Where to run first? Whom could I trust with my secret? Who wouldn't tell? Who would, or could actually *hide* me for a while? Was there anyone? Were there any friends who wouldn't *judge* me? What, exactly would, or could I tell them? How much, or how little of the truth should I share? What if they didn't believe me? What if they thought I brought this upon myself? Who in the hell could I ever confide in, especially after this total violation of my naïve trust in my so-called "friend" "L."? There's no one — nobody who could provide me a safe haven. I didn't even have any siblings, so I was totally...and utterly...alone.

Oh God! If only I could make any sense out of the questions plaguing my consciousness. If anything in my own known universe would ever make sense again — I certainly wondered. A sense of indescribable confusion and immeasurable anger osmosed throughout every cell of my violated being. I wondered how this man could have stolen, not only my body, but also my hopes, my dreams, my joy, my passion and my true innocence. And — for God's sake, what the hell could J.S. have been laughing at?

Chapter 6: What the Hell!!??

Suddenly, the sensation of movement just a few steps behind me in S.'s bedroom doorway, thrust my thoughts into rapid refocus. My muscles tightened, creating a tsunami of tension which rippled from my head to my toes. Too afraid to turn around, or even as much as squint in that direction, I clutched my cocooning sheet and pulled it tighter around me. Another shudder traveled across my skin. I felt very dizzy and everything seemed to be happening in slow motion, as if there were a five-second, out-of-sync delayed disconnect between each of my thoughts.

My feet were so firmly planted in the miniscule forest of blue carpet fibres, I could not take one step in any direction. Then, just at the instant I began to sense the room spinning, I felt a man's hands touch me from behind — one grasping each bare shoulder, (the only part of my flesh just barely exposed). I *knew* it was J.S. — back for *more*! As the adrenaline shot through me, my mouth felt dry, my pulse quickened and my heart raced. Yet, although it was a blisteringly hot day, I was in such a state of shock I was unable to sweat. Was *he* returning to KILL ME? Could this possibly happen with so many "witnesses" right downstairs? My legs seemed to dissolve into fleshy pools and I suddenly sensed this must be what dying would feel like. Feeling as if I were about to faint, I braced in anticipation of what seemed to be an impending certainty, in the very least — a *repeated rape*!

As I lowered my eyes, I glanced at my right shoulder and noticed this was not *his* massive hand. It was considerably smaller and much paler. These were hands which seemed to be offering a comforting caress. Slowly they guided me around until I found myself face-to-face, not with J.S., but with a different man. I all but shrieked with relief and silently thanked my God that it was *only* S. I knew that S. was not one of *them*. He was not a jock. He was not into sports, not into beer and I was reasonably reassured at that moment knowing he was rumoured to even be "not into women". Though it was common knowledge that S. was a "druggie" and a "pot-head", his laid-back attitude and apparent lack of testosterone-fueled aggression, made his presence in the room seem to pose no threat to me whatsoever. Also, I'd heard that, as an artist, he was some sort of creative genius, a label which I mistakenly equated with a sort of brilliant intellectualism.

Everyone knew S. was a true artist — an accomplished painter *and* a sculptor. It was *his* bedroom I was standing in, and the room where he obviously displayed his very best work — the same painting responsible for placing me in that doorway in the first place. I believed this student's parents travelled a lot, or at least they worked a great deal, leaving S., who was probably around eighteen, home alone much of the time. Of course, I'd never been there before, but it was common knowledge that a crowd of different kids regularly frequented his place. It was rumoured to be a kind of drop-in hangout with a "revolving door" of friends and acquaintances continually coming and going. I had heard kids even crashed there to avoid returning to their own homes and risk getting busted for being drunk, stoned or high from one illegal hard drug or another. But, to me these were only rumours and had never borne any relevance, since personally I was not part of his crowd. I had *never* taken any drugs, *never* touched a drink of alcohol, nor did I hang out with hippies.

I'm sure on the surface, most parents would only see S. as a "long-haired-hippie-freak". Personally I had no preconceived notions or apprehensions whatsoever. But, my mind *was* relieved a little as I thought he might be the *friend* who would help me escape the awful mess I was in. (Curiously the thought had not yet occurred to me as to S.'s whereabouts while J.S. had been attacking me. I just didn't have the presence of mind to wonder where S. had been during my struggling and screaming for help, since the sounds I made were obviously coming from behind *his own locked bedroom door.*)

S. said not a word while his heavy-lidded eyes read me from bottom to top. Carefully he adjusted my cocoon, gently easing it further up around my shoulders. I felt very safe — almost semi-OK. That's when he sat down in his father's handed-down, heavily shellacked, swivel desk chair, with the padded and brass-studded, black leather seat and back. Still, I remained unconcerned by his physical proximity. I was sobbing deeply from my toes, when quite unexpectedly he put his arms around my waist, pulling me very close, and pushing my head against his shoulder. He hugged me tightly, so tightly in fact that the air was completely squeezed out of my lungs and no utterances could escape from my mouth. Actually, his hug was painful to my abused body, but I needed *kind reassurance* more than anything just then, so I did not fight his grasp.

At that most vulnerable moment, my emotions were uncontrolled and spilling over their breakwall. I gasped a breath and began blubbering on to him about what had just occurred, as if I somehow felt that he had not been a witness within earshot, as all the other men downstairs had certainly been. I actually believed that most definitely he couldn't have been in the house while I was being attacked. Nevertheless, S. continued holding me tightly with *apparent* caring and genuinely doled-out sympathy. A moment later, he actually began to cry with me in so excruciating and painful a manner that he appeared to share in the experience of my anguish. Strangely enough, I felt as if I should be comforting *him*. S. kept repeating, "God, I'm so sorry—sorr—just *so* sorry!" and, "I didn't know that *this* was going to happen! How *could* I know this? It's just that, well, once J. started, you know, *I* was helpless to stop it. You sure didn't deserve this. But I couldn't help you and I'm so sorry."

[It was at that exact moment I realized that, indeed S. had also been present in the house, along with the other *men*. No doubt he heard the scuffling and my screams and cries of protest as I struggled to fight off J.S.'s assault.]

Chapter 7: No, *I'm* So Sorry!

I was so distracted by S.'s actions, I found myself profoundly apologizing for the bloodied sheets — **his** sheets! My God, it's so absurd when you think about the gravity of my desperate situation and yet my concern was for those expensive sheets. Then S. said what I believe he thought would comfort me, that he would "just toss them", and that his "mother" would "never miss them". However, his suggestion had the opposite effect of making the sheets seem almost like an inanimate representation of myself. I was feeling as if I were used merchandise, damaged goods, torn, bloodied and destined to be tossed into the trash, perhaps even incinerated! After all, who in the world would ever miss me, my sweet innocence, or whatever I may have been destined to become in this lifetime — that is, if I could ever live through the lifelong effects from this horrendous, rape and somehow be permitted to mature in life?

The other questions married to this one were, of course, "Who would ever want a girlfriend, a woman or a wife who had either *allowed* herself to be have sex before marriage, or put herself in a position to be raped?" or else, "Who would date a girl who really *wanted to* bed this so-called football hero?" For that matter, what man would ever *believe* me when, upon his discovery that I could not meet his expectations as a virginal woman? I would be forced to confess to no longer being pure and chaste, and would I be thought a liar if I tried to explain that my lost innocence was not through any fault of my own?

Still, S. had not yet turned loose of me, in fact, his "hug" had become even more constricting. He continued sobbing with me as he laid his head against my chest, against my small breasts, with only the thickness of the cocoon — a now *disposable* membrane, between us. Of course he was still sitting in the chair, with his legs apart, as men often tend to do. Then he stood me like a huge mound of molding clay between his knees. I clearly remember his kind words, "You need to get dressed and I'll get you on home. Oh, yeah and give me that bloody sheet so I can get rid of it — burn it or something."

Since nothing about S. had given me cause for alarm, certainly his sexual preference for men was, in the very least, reassuring for me at that vulnerable moment. So, obligingly I emerged from my cocoon, though far from a butterfly, still I was metamorphosed, just not in any *good* way. I leaned back, turned and eased toward the doorway where J.S. had hurriedly tossed my clothes aside. Then I was not more than a step away from my "rescuer" when he spun me around and pulled me back down, forcing me to straddle his now *closed* legs. Considering my overwhelming mental state, it never occurred to me to glance down as he pulled me nearer. Instead I thought I was getting just one more, much appreciated, though a little too forceful, hug from this gentle, sensitive human being. In that instant, it had totally slipped my mind that he was, after all, still a *male*. Nonetheless, I simply didn't think to try resisting him. Why should I, or would I?

Just then, S. gripped my bare hips directing them down onto his lap. My God! Oh My God!! He had *that look* — that same look in his eyes. It was the look which had pierced me as it emanated, not twenty minutes before, from J.S.'s eyes when it became branded into my brain during my life-altering and still immediately fresh, RAPE! Just then, very suddenly, S. "frenched" me, never releasing his tight grip of my bare hips. I was bewildered, bloodied, dazed and sticky with J.S.'s cum. I began whimpering like an orphaned puppy. Uncomfortably and awkwardly, I looked down in an attempt to push him away. I was perplexed and confused at the sight of his erect penis searching for a warm, willing receptacle — any receptacle — *MY RECEPTACLE!*

As I started to struggle for my freedom, suddenly I felt the stabbing knives and pressure of yet another forceful entry further violating my limp, broken body, and with it my rapidly withering spirit. Now it was purportedly *gay* S., my would-be, sort-of friend and saviour, who was making that physical connection which all straight teenage boys must think of every waking and sleeping moment of their lives! What the hell could he have been thinking? I was speechless and still exhausted and overwhelmed from fighting off my *first* rapist's forcible entries. This was different though, S. was not laughing at me. Instead it seemed as if he were simply experimenting with a female. However, he was doing so at the expense of my already broken, battered body and naïve young psyche — or what remained of these shattered pieces of *me*.

Perhaps, at best, he had to be thinking that with me in such a vulnerable state I would certainly welcome a second, more caring demonstration of *affection*. Or could his intentions have been much darker? Did he simply consider me a whore who was "just asking for it — asking to be raped"? Fearfully, I wondered if his mind, altered or numbed by drugs, was determined to enjoy some "sloppy seconds". Or was he thinking that forcing sex on me at that moment would simply be easy? Certainly there would be no resistance either from me, or from the remains of my virginal membrane, the ripped shreds from which, now painted *his* white sheets red, (*both* having been split apart and redesigned with a bloody brush). But S. was not only trying to penetrate me with his penis, but was also smothering me with his reeking, rotting-teeth-marijuana-flavoured mouth suffocating mine!

Fortunately, S. was not nearly as big, or muscular a man as the lumbering, cowardly felon who had just ripped through every part of my existence. So I concentrated, focusing on the adrenaline-driven fear and anger which were welling-up inside of me. I was able to push myself away, "unplugging" him, as it were, from my mouth and my vagina simultaneously. I grabbed the bloody top sheet, again threw it toga-style around myself, and swept up my clothes from the bedroom doorway. Then, I'm positive that without once touching the floor, I virtually flew into the small bathroom which, from S.'s bedroom doorway, was the next door to the right, adjacent off the hallway. I locked the doorknob and prayed the lock would hold against all the evils accosting me from other side of it.

Once safely in there, I cowered in the small, stuck-in-the-thirties, green-and-black tiled, temporary sanctuary. After I shed my cocoon, I stood quietly in the tub, mesmerized as I watched the bloody streams once again snake around my legs and trickle onto my feet. Absolutely in a daze, I numbly witnessed as so much of my life's essence was dripping, draining, going, and then gone in that one fractured instant. However, I couldn't understand why I was bleeding so much. With the faucet water swishing my blood trails from the shiny green tub surface, I understood that it was the blood — my blood and not the water, which was the final cleansing flow, washing J.S.'s sticky filth off, and out, of me.

"Mary...c'mon out here!

Fuck, I'm sorry baby.

It was stupid.

I promise I won't hurt you now.

C'mon out!

Give me that bloody shit so I can get rid of it before my ol' lady gets home!

Baby—wanna Coke? [6]

Baaaaaa-by! ... Hey, d'ya wanna Coke?"

A Coke? ***A Coke?*** Geeze — how the hell was *that* gonna change what had already transpired with J.S. and now with what S., himself, had attempted? And about the name "Baby", I was neither S.'s, nor J.S.'s nor anyone else's "Baby" — except, my Daddy's of course. And the *child* that I had existed upon my arrival at this hell-house, well *she **was** no longer!* How dare this asshole so feebly attempt to endear himself to me with a Coke? My God! He hardly even knew my name!

Chapter 8: I've Gotta Git Outta This Place...

That was the turning point for me. Quickly I found myself refocusing and welling-up with anger at this man — no, not a "man", but just one more *coward*. Indeed he was a coward, a phoney and a sheepish fake in hippie's clothing. I couldn't believe the abject cruelty S. had displayed by trying to sneak in through the back door of my being! It seems as if he'd been intent upon some sort of "soft" rape, (J.S. having already *laid* the ground work, so to speak.) Had this entire second act, this segue, not been so pathetically absurd, it might have been terrifying. All I could think of was, "why?... Why?... WHY?... and **WHY ME**?!" Who were these men and how the hell did they get so wrong an opinion of who I really was ... and what I really wasn't??!!

As I quickly wiped the blood and semen off my broken, battered body, I found my thoughts drifting to Jesus Christ who was crucified and nailed on the cross at Calvary. Yes, decidedly, I thought, although pure, sinless and innocent, when Jesus was crucified, His precious broken body would have created many, many more bloody rivers of innocence plundered. Bolstered up a little thinking about Jesus, I felt a little less alone. I tried to wash my face and the inside of my mouth to get rid of the taste and smell of J.S.'s disgusting ejaculate and the loathsome reminders of both his beer-flavoured, and S.'s marijuana-flavoured, mouths. Quickly I re-dressed myself, stuffing a big rolled-up wad of toilet tissue inside my panties to sop-up the still-trickling blood. I never answered S. who was speaking through my sanctuary door, limply trying to make right, that which he had so seriously fouled up.

Fearfully, and patiently, I waited an eternity behind that green bathroom door. I waited so long in fact, I heard a few different guys complaining about having to "take a piss out in the backyard". It wasn't until I could hear no more sounds, no more laughter, no more clanking beer bottles or clacking billiard balls that I was able to quietly, gingerly ease out of my sanctuary. Not too far though, only just a little way. This time I had to be completely certain of my safety. After scanning the small hallway and determining that S.'s bedroom was empty, I tip-toed across the hall and glanced into the kitchen on my right. On my left, it was a straight shot, down three steps to the small landing inside the back door on the right. But it terrified me as I remembered there were only four more steps making an L-shape going down into the infamous rec-room on the left.

Why was everyone so quiet? I determined from the voices that most of the guys were still down there — in fact, I could *smell* them. Were they waiting for me to attempt my escape, only to grab me as I run past? Or, I wondered if they might be waiting right outside the back door, ready to slam it in my face and slap me back into that iniquitous den. Though petrified with fear, I began admonishing myself for not paying closer attention to the layout of the rest of the house. Suddenly, in that quiet moment I realized men's voices, now speaking in hushed tones, were coming from the *living room*. Dazed and stunned, I crouched down, waiting to see who might next be coming after me. I recognized the voices as J.S.'s and S.'s, but there was someone else. Was it R.'s? Yes, I thought it sounded like R.'s voice.

The pot smoke, which fairly reeked like barbequed manure, was quite overwhelming my senses and really doing a number on my asthmatic lungs. I desperately needed to cough hard and expel the smoke, but I couldn't risk betraying my whereabouts. What if those men were waiting in the living room to prevent me from escaping in that direction, in order to rape me yet again and again — all of them? Suddenly my heart fairly leapt from my chest, as someone banged on the back screened door loudly enough for it to rattle in and out, creating a double-knocking sound. I was still cowering in the hall and couldn't see around the corner, when I heard some guy holler through the screen, "Hello … hello … hey …hey...Pizza...Pizza delivery!" Loud footsteps alerted me that someone was starting up the stairs from the game-room, then J.S. hollered from the living room, "I've got it! Hey man, hey S. gimme seven bucks!" [Incidentally I'd heard rumours that S. was dealing drugs like marijuana, LSD, MDA and STP. It made sense too, because later I would discover that S. always, *always* seemed to have a wad of cash on him — a *big fat wad*!]

Almost crawling, I quickly slipped back into my green hide-out. As I peered through the slivered opening of the bathroom door, which I hadn't yet completely closed, I saw J.S. take two or three long strides from the kitchen. His weight actually vibrated through the floor. S. was directly behind him waving two *fins*, [five-dollar bills], to cover the difference. Though my rapist never saw me from the hall, my would-be rapist, S., looked directly at me — no, actually right through the door-sliver and *right through me*. I'll never forget the look in his eyes. It was clearly one of disdain and disgust aimed directly into, and received by, my broken soul.

Chapter 9: My Great Escape

Within the security of the curiously *dated* little bathroom, once again I locked-out the world of darkness and evil, or at least I attempted to. I hadn't actually *seen* the owner of the *third* 'voice', [R.'s], but I heard him, and felt the vibrations of his weight, as he dogged the other two from the living room. When he emerged from the kitchen eating pizza as he walked, R. didn't look in the direction of my green sanctuary, so I'm guessing he never *saw* me either. At that point there was a flurry of activity, including a couple collisions as the guys ran up and down the steps, two and three steps at a time. The smell of those pizzas made me want to vomit, yet again — but I couldn't let them all know how completely devastated I was feeling at that moment. So, I held my breath, trying to withhold the vomit, suppress the asthma and stay invisible until I could think of a plan. However, when a cough was inevitable, I grabbed one of the two "guest towels", that are obviously for decoration and not ever really *used*, and I rolled it up tightly and coughed into it. Nevertheless, I couldn't stifle the pain in my head which felt as if it were splitting into a million pieces, all exploding in a thousand different directions.

When I no longer felt the slick, alternating white and black, octagonal ceramic tiled floor vibrating from all the men's lead-footed movements through the hall, I had to try once more to escape. J.S., S. and R. were back in the dining room scarfing pizza and talking, almost too quietly. I heard my name mentioned every so often, but couldn't exactly hear what they were saying. I was so afraid they were planning to break down the bathroom door, drag me out and all three of them rape me right there on the floor of that damned green broad-loomed hall! I knew I had to act very quickly and my only plan could be to go out that side door as unobtrusively as possible and hopefully be unnoticed. But as I listened to the movements of the old, dark-green, wood frame screen door, I observed that it had one of those really strong, and very noisy, spring-back hinges that everybody's dad loved to install, "to keep the flies out of the house". (From my personal experience of having my fingers caught in ours, I knew those springs would pull the screen door quickly shut, and always with a *very hard slam!* They could also flay the skin from any misfortunate fingers which happened to get in the way.)

I waited and listened as minutes morphed into eternities. The pool table downstairs, one corner of which was in direct line-of-sight to the back door, had fallen eerily silent. When I was able to hear slightly more than my heart banging in my ears, I made out the muffled voices of some game on TV. That, and the intermittent grunts, convinced me that everyone was either chowing-down on pizza, concentrating on the game, or at some stage of passing completely out from a combination of food and beer. In any event it sounded as if the men must be somewhat mellowed, and I could only pray that if they were about three sheets to the wind at that point, they'd be disinclined to move off their butts and chase after me.

A quick prayer for deliverance set my feet on angel's wings as my brain injected my heart with another huge shot of adrenaline. When my muscles responded, I sprang across the hall and, barely touching the three little steps, I was immediately at the screen door. I opened it quite gingerly and then, only far enough for my thin frame to squeeze through. As I slid out the door I was careful to hold it tightly, allowing it to close softly against my small fingers. Ahhhh ... not a sound, thanks to God and my angels, as I could afford no less than silence from that threatening door spring!

Immediately, from that house I was marathon-running, at least in my own mind, although the agony in my body obviously inhibited anywhere near such speedy movement. However, despite my weakness and nausea, I felt as if I *should be* running for my life. Nevertheless, I could, and did, walk as fast as I ever had, or at least as fast as the continually increasing stabbing pains in my raw vagina would permit. Nevertheless, I was determined to *never* look back, not even for a split second, because I knew the *face* I would be looking at would be the ***devil's***.

My mind was riddled with questions of what I could possibly do next. Of course, I could *not* go to the police. I was certain *their* collective attitude would probably imply that I "*asked for it*", or I somehow "*deserved it*". After all, the police were *men* too! And I certainly could not go home to my parents, for fear of upsetting and hurting my Daddy. Nor could I confess to my minister, as he would be obliged to tell the police, my parents, the principal, the crossing-guard, newspaper boy ... *Oh, My God!* ... I realized the extensive, winding grapevines investigating my horrible truths would be endless — and timeless.

I genuinely feared for my life and the lives of my elderly parents. After all, who knew of what heinous atrocities such a man as *J.S.* was capable, or even how far his cronies would go to protect *him,* and *themselves*, from anything I might "allege" they did to me? I could think of no one to trust with such a *terrible secret*, especially after my trust, as I will explain shortly, had already been so cruelly and unexpectedly dishonoured and violated.

Chapter 10: No Place to Run…

When I had made it far enough away and could see I was not being pursued, I realized I had already reached the opposite side of nearby T. M. Park. I was actually surprised by the normalcy I witnessed as I glanced around at folks enjoying their regular Saturday afternoon family activities. A girl about five, in pink shorts and pigtails, was struggling and fighting with her little brother who was rubbing her dolly in the dirt. Two other little girls were pumping hard, trying to beat each other's height on the swings. Two boys were each banging down hard, in turn on the teeter-totter, and were giggling their heads off. A father was trying to teach his daughter to find her balance on her shiny new red two-wheeler which was now minus the training wheels that he'd just removed. And four other children were in the sandbox playing with colourful plastic pails, shovels and sand molds. No one in the park that day was acting in any unusual way at all. Every person I could see was oblivious to the fact that *my* entire life had just been raped-away in a little bungalow, which I could almost see on the far side of the park. Nobody even noticed me.

Exhausted from my rape, my physical struggles with J.S. and my emotional fight with S., not to mention from the loss of blood, I needed to rest. I couldn't go home, not yet anyway. As I glanced around the park, my first thought was to hide in the public washroom. It was a small, rectangular, cinderblock building with a green shingled roof and two dark green painted wooden door entrances, separating the BOYS' side from the GIRLS'. However, as I got nearer to it, its reeking stench of urine and disinfectant cakes, combined with the blistering summer heat, forced the vomit to creep back up into my throat.

Suddenly, I realized I was feeling a wetness between my legs and I was afraid the wad of toilet paper had already become saturated with blood and was leaking its contents down my thighs. I had to hide somewhere, immediately! It was at that exact moment I noticed a little black Scottie dog with a red-leather collar. He was chasing a red-white-and-blue rubber ball all the way under a cluster of evergreen trees which framed the perimeter of the park's grassy play area. My attention was then drawn to one extremely large tree and I understood what I had to do.

Chapter 11: A Place to Hide...

I felt a small measure of comfort as I imagined this titan must have overseen and protected its park for at least *fifty times* as many years as I had even been alive. Surely it could disguise and protect me. I could only hope as much anyway. I was determined to take refuge and solace by crawling under the lowest and longest of its sweeping, swaying branches skirting the bottom of its trunk. The tips of those branches had, over time, kissed a barren, circular patch, directly behind the uncut grass and needle-laden ring around the evergreen's circumference. It made an ideal hiding place, even if only temporary. Once underneath, I leaned back against the rough, firm, gray-brown trunk. As a small breeze caressed the tree limbs, immediately the tree whispered its acceptance of this little refugee from life,

"*Safe...safe...safe...safe...safe...*"

(But, how did it know?)

I tried to just breathe — not to *catch* my breath — to take my *first real breath* since escaping the iniquity in S.'s house. Then my tears began to flow and did so until no more tears would come. I'm certain that on that fateful, life-changing day, nobody even noticed the little girl, (and I *was* only a little girl), sheepishly cowering and sobbing under the evergreen tree. I suppose I should have felt angrier for the violations inflicted upon me. Instead, however, I felt very small and stupid, embarrassed, ugly, dirty, nasty and pathetic — all multiplied by tens of thousands. I blamed *myself*, as I had always been in the habit of doing, and then I questioned how the hell I had ended up in this drama in the first place. I mulled back over the incidents that got me to that *den of iniquity,* and I asked myself,

"*Why did I go to help my friend L.?*"

"*Why did I go inside, when 'the girls weren't yet back from the store'?*"

"*Why did I go upstairs with J.S.?*"

... and when the cigarette and pot smoke were choking me so badly ...

"*Why didn't I leave the house completely?*"

"Why was I so naïve, so dumb to think J.S. was actually only making polite conversation with me? Did I think this 'jock' was just trying to be nice and make me feel more comfortable by escorting me around S.'s house while I awaited the girls' return?"

*"Whatever made me think for a second that 'J.S.-the-Jock' would be interested in art — S.'s art, and would want to share this passion for creativity by giving **me** a personal tour of the house?"*

"How could I be so stupid, so naïve, as to not see it was the classic, 'come up and see my etchings' scenario?"

Naturally, this is crystal clear in retrospect, but why couldn't I have known it all before that fateful day?!!

****

Yes, of course, I was *safe*. Perhaps I could stay there *forever*. I *had* to stay there if I were to remain *safe. Forever — why couldn't I, or shouldn't I?* I tried to straighten-out my clothes and once again pulled my long, sun-bleached, fair hair back into its ingenuous ponytail. As I retrieved the two Cover Girl [10] items from my diminutive, soft white leather purse, I became focused on the pretty way it was so delicately hand-crafted and decorated with the Indian fringe and very tiny, colourful beading in a sunray pattern. My mind drifted to the day my Daddy bought it for me, when we were out on one of our regular day-trips to Niagara Falls. Of course, the face powder and a little rouge pot were the only items of makeup which, at fourteen, I was permitted to use, (certainly I was not allowed to use any lipstick or mascara). So, with those two items I tried to freshen-up my face, enough to disguise my pain before I got home. I was just trying to make myself "right enough" on the outside to be able to face my wonderful, loving, kindly Daddy. (I knew I could never let him suspect for one second that any such harm had befallen me, his "Little Bunny", his so-called "perfect little girl".)

No, there would be no one *ever* whom I could trust. I had to make all evidence of the rape disappear, including the evidence of the wretched smells and the vile tastes still assaulting my senses. But how could I disguise the distant, vacant, *thousand mile stare* which my shattered soul beamed back at me from the sad, blue-eyed reflection in the little, round compact's mirror?

Chapter 12: I Still Have to Go Home

From the fragrant safety of my *new* green hideout, I waited solemnly for a very long time. I waited until I could no longer freshly sense the weight of J.S.'s clumsy body on top of me. I waited until the wafting scent of my evergreen's *arms* erased the memory of the stench of J.S.'s breath and his stinking semen on my face ... and in my *mouth*! I waited until my soul was *almost* restored, though not entirely safely interred within my body's rudely violated shell. I waited until my wafting, waving, resplendent sanctuary hushed that the time had come for me to leave. Eventually, when I heard, *"Yessss...Yessss...Yessss..."* I knew the gentle breeze, which softly ruffled through the brilliant green needles, was finally whispering its permission for me to exit.

During my reverent contemplation under the safety of that towering evergreen, my mind started to wander. It drifted far enough, until I began questioning where on earth *I* had gone wrong. I still couldn't understand how circumstances had placed me in such a compromised position. Exactly how did I get into such a horrible mess? What the hell was I even doing over at S.'s house in the first place? I played back the mental tapes of my conversation with L. in order to decipher if any *red flags* should have tipped me off. I recalled that she had phoned me earlier that Saturday, crying frantically; in fact, she was almost hysterical.

Chapter 13: "L." Needs Me

"Mar..."

"Oh! Oh! Hey, L. ... is D. ... I mean I heard ... well are you ... OK?"

"No, no — not really, not at all. Oh God, Mar, I'm going crazy. D. is soooo messed up. You know, he'll NEVER be able to walk — ever, not EVER again! He won't even wake up, Mar. Oh my God, it's like he's dead. I really thought he was, but he's not ... at least not yet. I know he can't hear me. I can't even talk to him, or hug him. God, Mar ... I just can't stop throwing up. What can I do? What should I do?!!"

Her voice was so shaky and I could tell she was sobbing. Personally, I'd never experienced such a tragedy, although I *could* empathize with her fear that she would lose the one person she *loved the most*. After all, I had lived every day of my life, since elementary school, wondering if *this* would be the day that I came home to no longer hearing my Daddy's struggling, strangled breaths and his violent, wrenching coughing emanating from the upstairs bedroom. He suffered so greatly as the thieving emphysema slowly robbed him of his health, and sooner than I would ever imagine, of his life ...

I knew my "friend" L. had to be going totally out of her mind! I would have been a real basket-case if I were facing similar circumstances. I just tried to control my voice and sound calm and reassuring. That seemed to be what she needed from me at that moment. (It was common knowledge that *I* was the friend who could always be counted on to offer a solid shoulder on which to lean, and someone trustworthy enough to keep even the darkest secrets secure. *"If you tell Mar, it won't go anywhere!"*)

I couldn't help thinking about how tight she and D. were. I imagined them to be as close as any siblings could hope to be — no, actually even closer. They were each other's best friends. Heck, they even hung out together, and what siblings ever hang around together? L. was always so private, and closed-up. She usually shared secrets *only* with her brother, at least up until that tragic time in their lives.

We had only just begun the ninth grade, but I think D. was in tenth. He made no effort to hide the fact that he was quite *sweet* on *me*. D. wanted so badly to be my boyfriend, even going so far as to secretly hand-deliver small gifts to my doorstep. Once he brought me a fancy little, partially used, sea-green tinted, solid, roll-up style perfume in a little gold-coloured tube, (no doubt, at that point, missing from his mom's boudoir). Another gift was a pretty lipstick in a lipstick-sized bejeweled case, with its own mirror! It was also a little *used*, and was a bright Revlon Red [12] colour, also befitting one's '"mother's' style. In fact, I was certain she would have been missing this item from her dressing table as well. D. just wouldn't accept that, at the time, I was quite smitten with the boy I had been sort-of *dating*, E., or as he was known to his friends, "Sticks", (though I never understood why).

Two nights prior to L.'s call, D. had been in a devastating car wreck. The family was notified that the prognosis appeared terribly grave. I had already heard that D. *wasn't expected to live*; but if by some miracle he pulled through, he would be a *quadriplegic* — possibly a "*vegetable*" was the term they actually used, [obviously prior to enforcement of 'political correctness' in such circumstances]. But what did these strange, frightening terms really mean?

I knew from the tone of the conversation that L. had no idea that I had already been privy to the most thorough description of D.'s car accident. So, acting as if first hearing it, I politely listened in silence as she related the graphic details of the wreck. I never indicated that my phone had been ringing non-stop, as all our mutual friends wanted to share the news with me, since everyone was aware, of course, how D. felt about *me*.

At that moment L. needed a trustworthy friend and a shoulder on which to cry. Ironically enough, despite the fact that I was not part of her tight-knit *clique* of BFF girlfriends, she trusted *me* to be that friend! I continued to listen as this girl choked on her tear-drenched words. A dreadful sensation washed over me. I was helpless realizing how devastated she was. I could almost share the depth of her heartache, so much so that *I* too felt like vomiting as she imparted more particulars about the devastation which the tragic wreck was imposing on herself and her family.

Nevertheless, I started wondering what on earth *I* could possibly do to help her that her *usual* friends could not. But when she asked me to meet with her to talk, of course my instinctive reply was,

"Are you gonna be home for a while L., 'cause I'll come right over?"

"Thanks, Mar ... Yes, I want you to come over, but, um, but I'm not actually at home, I'm at S.'s place."

"S. who?"

"S. You know!"

"What? You don't mean S., that hippie guy? What are you doing over there?" I wondered aloud.

"S. said it was OK if some of my girlfriends got together over here to try and help me get my mind off D. I had to get away from my house 'cause it was sooooo depressing watching my mum cry all the time."

"Of course, OK, well, it doesn't matter where you're at, L., I'm on my way."

"Come to the back door, OK?"

Chapter 14: I'm On My Way

I knew S. was kind-of a strange guy. I guessed on this sunny Saturday afternoon he was just having another one of his usual *open houses*. Though I'd promised to be right over, it took me a little while to figure out what to tell my parents, because I was not allowed to go to anyone's house that they didn't know. So I lied and said I needed to meet L. at her place, and of course, they trusted me implicitly, and bought my story, as usual. [I was well-practiced at the art of fabricating stories, often having to deceive my adoptive parents in order to do anything I ever wanted to do! They were just so over-protective, and, of course, I always believed that their overly-strict rules, such as the prescript that I couldn't be friends with a "Catholic", were completely out of left field and definitely unfair!] Nevertheless, this was my *first* mistake.

It certainly didn't take me long to change my clothes, or to cut out a few of the four or five blocks over to S.'s house, by crossing through T. M. Park. But honestly, I wasn't really looking forward to spending the afternoon chatting with L.'s "real" girlfriends, a little group *I* didn't fit into. Besides that, I knew it would be tough trying to comfort L. Nonetheless, I chose to ignore the tiny voice in my head whispering a warning that something didn't feel quite right about L. asking me to meet her at S.'s, and at the *back* door, no less. All I really remember is feeling somewhat pleased that she trusted, perhaps respected, and really seemed to *need* me at that vulnerable time in her life.

In no time I approached S.'s house and headed around back to the screened door. I noticed that the door's dark green paint was peeling badly, revealing several years of the homeowners' attempts at changing exterior house colours. I was just about to knock when I was startled by a large, hulking man who was shadowed, standing just inside! Curiously, I wondered if he had actually been watching me through the rusted screen as I neared the back door. His presence struck me as very odd since I knew he wasn't S. and I wondered why he, and not L., was waiting at the door. I figured that certainly this huge guy was at least in grade thirteen, which, at that time in Ontario high schools, was the highest grade prior to matriculation.

When the man insisted that I "C'mon in.", I silently questioned what on earth he was doing there. I knew he was too young to be a parent, too tall, too big overall to be S., and if I understood L. correctly, it was going to be an afternoon *only with the girls*. Naturally, I was feeling very nervous, embarrassed and suddenly shy, recognizing I was actually talking to a senior from our high school.

I stammered that I was there "to ... to ... to meet L." and that she'd "asked me to come over and talk". Then I asked him flat out,

"Isn't she here?" and he replied,

"She just left with the girls to pick up some more Cokes and chips. They'll be back any minute. She said for you to just wait in the house."

I replied that, "I'd prefer to wait out here on the stoop."

But, once again he urged,

"It's OK, it's too hot out there, just come on in and wait here for the girls."

It seemed like a harmless enough suggestion, but this assumption would be my *second* mistake that day. I noticed this man spoke quite softly for someone of his stature, perhaps a "gentle giant", I presumed. So I nodded affirmatively and he pushed the screen door out towards me. Then he repeated, in a somewhat more demanding tone, "*C'mon in!*" So I did. However, my natural response to his seemingly innocent invitation, became not only the turning point, but also, the biggest mistake of my entire life, either before, or so far, after that day. As I stepped over the threshold I asked the young man,

"Is L. OK?"

But he never replied. Then, stepping under his outstretched arm as he held the open door, I entered the house. However, in the moment I did so, he suddenly let go of the screen door! It quickly slammed shut behind me, hitting my bum and knocking my face straight into his chest — virtually into his arms, since he had, as yet, neither turned, stepped away, nor descended into the rec-room.

My gosh! I was soooo embarrassed, though *he* seemed not phased in the least. "You can wait down there." he insisted, pointing sort-of the way a hitch-hiker would, with a thumb over his shoulder. I reiterated that I was only there to meet-up with L. Though his face had an odd expression which was impossible to read, he said nothing more to me. His thumb simply repeated its indication for me to go on down to the game room. I said, "Uh, I'm Mary...." and, cutting me off, he just nodded again, indicating he knew who I was, and my purpose in being there. He never offered his name, but I had already recognized him as a student from my high school. Nevertheless, in a very short time I would discover that he was "J.S.", though it certainly didn't matter to me one way or another, since I was really only there for L.

Weeks later I discovered J.S. was an "important" football player at school, and was likely his team's "Captain", or at least a "quarterback", whatever that meant. In any case, I did understand he was somehow "famous" and important in our school's hierarchy of sports players. He was a very, very big guy — virtually towering all of my ninety-one pounds which, incidentally were fitted quite snugly on my petite 5'1" frame. In any event, he was obviously much older and certainly bigger than me, by far. Of that much I was certain, when my face was pushed into his chest by the tight door spring slamming shut against my bum!

I guessed I was being ushered to the game room so as not to disturb S.'s parents, whom I assumed were at home upstairs, (my *third* mistake that day). Since this man was standing firmly on the little landing, I was forced to squeeze past him, tip-toeing cautiously down the four fateful steps. I couldn't help but notice that the loud, alternating argumentative and laughing voices rising from the basement, were obviously not being made by any girls at all. (I thought if any had stayed behind while the others did the "Coke run", they weren't making a sound.) I felt quite uneasy about descending to the rec-room. I only wanted to make myself as unobtrusive as possible. I really didn't want to be there. I wasn't feeling comfortable at all, but I had been raised too politely to be "rude," and just push past him and leave. (Ah yes, my *fourth* mistake.)

Chapter 15: Testosterone Netherworld

Sensing this man's body heat as he followed closely against my back, I started feeling increasingly nervous. I was trembling so violently on the inside, I could only hope it wasn't visible on the outside. The "men", (and they definitely seemed like *men* to me and certainly not just high school kids), were all down there playing billiards or watching some lame sports game on the console TV, a set which was sitting low on the floor, in a brown wooden "hi-fi" type of housing. It was obvious that all of them were drinking beer, or something else obviously "alcoholic". In my thirteen years of life, I had only witnessed a few people who imbibed anything alcoholic. One was my adoptive "mother", who favoured Mogen David's kosher Jewish table and Passover wine [11]. Because she was an Anglican Protestant, I never understood why she chose this brand, except probably because it was the biggest bottle for the smallest price! (Of course, I never saw my Daddy's lips touch alcohol.)

[The only others in my life who partook of alcoholic beverages, were my adult cousins, my "Mother's" brother's children, down in Woodstock, Ontario, all of whom I witnessed guzzling beer like water when they played all-night poker in my Uncle C.'s basement.]

Naturally, I only wanted *not* to be noticed by those older guys; after all, I had only *just turned fourteen*. Also, I was suddenly very shy, especially around those large football-types, who were down there doing their "guy-stuff". I hoped no one would speak to me because I wouldn't know what to say. I felt out-numbered, out-classed, out of place and waaaaaay out of my safety zone! Since I didn't drink alcohol, watch TV sports or shoot pool, the best I could do, while I awaited the girls' return, was to make myself invisible! [This was a talent, at which I had become quite adept, or so I believed. I had years' of practice, due to the necessity of hiding my *real self* away from people, so as not to reveal the result of horrible daily abuse and molestation inflicted upon me by my so-called "Mother", (my "adoptive 'mother'" who was galaxies away from my "real" "mother".)]

Trying to look anywhere but at the young men, I studied the layout and furnishings of the basement recreation room. I noticed the odd arrangement of the two sofas, neither of which sported any legs. One faced towards the large combination "hi-fi" stereo and console TV set to the right of the stairs and the other was on the left, lengthwise, parallel to, and facing the length of the pool table.

As my eyes adjusted to the darkened room I noticed the TV chesterfield was well worn-in, with cushions pancaked by the weighty jack-hammering of TV sports fans' bums. It could've easily held three average-sized people, but was completely filled with only two of these humongous guys! One of the tube-watchers was R., my so-called "boyfriend" E.'s, "Sticks'", older brother, a guy I was pretty certain was also on the football team.

Walking straight ahead along the narrow path between the TV sofa and the near end of the billiards table, I noticed that the lights suspended over the pool table, were the only ones turned on at the time. It was the TV screen that was illuminating the rest of what seemed to be a windowless room. I recognized a big *coffee* table which was serving as a foot rest. It barely revealed the colour of its stain, under the four massive feet, multitude of beer bottles and, almost apologetically, the odd Coca Cola bottle.

I was instructed to sit down on the second "bleacher" which was a fuzzy, faded, orange-toned, floral, over-stuffed chesterfield. I sank down at one end grasping tightly to the wooden arm, so as to avoid being completely ingested by the sofa cushions! The entire expanse of that couch was empty except for one guy, with an open beer still in hand, which was balancing precariously on his belly against his belt buckle. He was completely passed out and hanging sideways over the opposite arm.

I could easily see the TV from the sofa, but because I always found TV sports terribly boring, I focussed on the goings-on at the billiards table. I was still trying to make myself small, unnoticeable, unseen — NOT there — INVISIBLE. Fortunately, no one seemed to really notice me — and NOBODY spoke to me or even made eye contact.

A couple guys were standing around the impressive, gargantuan, green felt-covered billiards table that virtually occupied the remainder of the room. Collectively, the guys in that rec-room all appeared to be engrossed in either shouting at the game on TV, or arguing about whose shot was next, while using *english* to throw the impossible spread of colourful, clacking billiard balls!

Glancing past the pool table, over in the corner I noticed an undersized refrigerator which had certainly seen better days. I understood why there were grumblings in the room about "warm beer". That fridge couldn't possibly have kept the beer cold, since I witnessed its door being opened far longer than it was shut! Inside it, I thought I noticed, concealed behind the brown beer bottles, the familiar red label of a Coke bottle or two, but I couldn't say with absolute certainty.

Invisible as I knew I had become, I had no intentions of speaking up, or even walking across the room to hunt for a soft drink in that fridge. Even when I needed to use the bathroom, I was too afraid and embarrassed to speak up and ask anyone where it was located. So patiently, motionlessly and barely breathing because of the smoke, I waiting for the girls to return.

[At this point I was convinced I had succeeded at achieving the virtually impossible — complete invisibility.]

I believe there were about seven or eight guys in total over there and the last one I noticed was sitting on top of the old deep freeze against the other wall. Though his face was shadowed, I saw the cue in his hand and knew he was just waiting for it to be his turn to wow the guys with his pool-shooting prowess. Although a little smaller than the others, his weight was still enough to cause the lid of that very large, steel appliance to bend down in the centre. (I supposed it had once sported a gleaming white enameled surface, but in its retirement had become yellowed, rust-blemished and stained from cigarette burns, or who knows what else.)

Just as my attention was drifting from my awkward position in that room, I was startled back to reality. One of the pool players, while picking a different cue, from the extras leaning against the wall, turned suddenly towards J.S. and accidentally knocked over all the cues. He complained,

"Hey man — what the hell is *she* doing here?"

He was tilting his head and pointing in my direction with the cue in his hand. (Oh my God! I was shocked to realize I hadn't actually become as "invisible" as I assumed I had!)

But J.S., who stood blocking the stairs, just glared at the guy and, with a shrug that I was unable to interpret, he gestured his response. Then J.S. asked me, "Mary, d'ya wanna beer?" "What!?" my mind replied. Then, reading the shock on my face he re-offered, "Or ... a Coke?" I nodded affirmatively in reply to the suggested cola, (I figured the noise level was too loud for me to be heard in that room anyway). "Wait right there!" he insisted, taking a few very long strides across to the fridge.

I saw him remove a red-labeled bottle and pour its contents into a glass. I remember thinking him a *gentleman* for not expecting me to crassly slug Cola straight out of the bottle like one of the guys. Though I couldn't be certain, I thought I noticed him pouring something else into the same glass. How amusing and un-cool I thought this big guy looked, handing me Coke in a Welches' Grape-jelly Flintstones' glass [13]. In any event, I thanked him politely and took a sip. However, I was shocked by my drink's vile flavour. It wasn't very cold so I figured that was the reason, or else it was flat, even so, it tasted nothing at all like Coca Cola, as I knew it. Not being one to complain though, I politely pretended to sip it, and then I resumed my invisible waiting. Besides, I mused, L. and the girls should be returning any second with those fresh Cokes; I'd just get one then.

[Of course, retrospective and life experience have demonstrated that drinks with an odd "medicine-y" after-taste contained some form of intoxicant such as cheap rum or whiskey. (This, of course, was prior to the trend nowadays of men more conveniently lacing girls' drinks with the so-called "date rape" drug "GHB" [14] — before committing their pre-planned heinous sexual molestation, battery, rape, or worse, murder.)]

At "half-time" or some other break in the televised game, I suggested to J.S. that I thought, "I'd better be leaving". J.S. was planted steadfastly, directly in front of me with his arms folded and feet wide apart. I giggled when this flesh-and-blood "Mr. Clean" [15], (looking just like the figure in the commercial, minus the bald head), was instructing me to "Wait a little longer — just a little longer." In any event, he really appeared silly to me in that moment.

A verrrrrry long time had passed when J.S. noticed I wasn't actually *drinking* my "Coke". He leaned down to me, commented that I looked awfully bored and asked if I would like to go upstairs and get a *real* Coke. (Ah ha! I knew there had been something wrong with my soda!) I *was* bored, and quite thirsty by then and my bladder was about to explode — so, naturally, I complied, (my *fifth* mistake that day).

[I should have left. I should have known. I should have seen it coming. But I didn't. I was young, naïve, inexperienced with worldly matters and, geeze am I kidding myself — I was just plain stupid. Hindsight, and only hindsight, is 20/20!]

So I agreed and followed J.S. up the four rec-room steps, then up the three steps to the little hallway, (just seven small steps into my destiny's altered state). As we approached the kitchen, I noticed the cluttered collage of pretzel bags, cans of nuts and potato chip bags littering the counter and most of them appeared quite full. Then J.S. reached into a fridge *full* of Cokes, and other soda pops; then he handed me an unopened Coke out of that fridge. Of course, it slowly dawned on me that there were plenty of snacks and drinks, and it really made no sense to me that all the girls went out to buy more.

Suddenly I seriously began feeling squirmy and most uncomfortable when J.S. started talking to me as if I were a *woman*. Was he actually flirting with me, or did I just imagine it? Not possible, I thought! I kept moving the conversation around to his relationship with his "beautiful fiancée — what's her name — is she with L.?" Nevertheless he kept averting that conversation. Instantly I wondered where the heck the girls really had gone, since there was certainly no shortage of Cokes or snacks of any kind! And considering the creepy way J.S. was speaking to me right there in the kitchen, I now wondered if S., or his parents, were even in the house at all.

Chapter 16: Come Up and See His Etchings!

The hook came when he said, "Have you ever seen S.'s art? It's all over the house. C'mon, I'll show you 'round." I thought whaaat?

"Um, I'm OK. You can just go back down there and I'll wait here for L."

"Naw, how about *a guided tour.*" he pressed. At that point, I was thinking that anything would be less uncomfortable than trying to reciprocate his *flirtatious, bordering on sexual,* conversation, so I said, "OK". Naïvely, though foolishly, I was ignoring the tiny voice in the back of my head telling me that this man did NOT seem the type to appreciate art in any form. (This was my *sixth* mistake that day.)

I eased slowly behind this hulk, moving through the kitchen to the adjacent dining room. Mounted over the buffet was one very large, multi-coloured, sort-of geometric, modernistic painting, the excellent quality of which frankly shocked me. The living room, to the right, off the dining room, boasted two more of these *interesting* paintings without apparent shape or form, but which incorporated a variety of colours, though predominantly black. On the floor beside the sofa was a very large "sculpting" of an unrecognizable, yet somewhat daunting, lump of something resembling a dark, shiny brown melted metal. My *guided tour* entailed my *appreciation* of two more of S.'s extraordinary avant-garde, cubist artistic accomplishments, which I sincerely found marvelous.

Then J.S. urged, "Let's go look in S.'s bedroom, he keeps his best one in there." At the time, that actually made sense to me, so we walked back through the kitchen and across the small hall where we faced S.'s open bedroom door. J.S. insisted, "Look there at the huge one over his bed." Not realizing that J.S. was *far* from an accomplished art critic, I suspended my better judgment and took his matter-of-fact comment at face value. Unaware of the significance and life-changing consequences awaiting me, I stepped over the threshold into the "netherworld" of my soon-to-be-violated innocence, (my *seventh* mistake in one day).

Yes, of course, J.S. was right. The largest and most impressive painting I had witnessed to date in my young life, disguised the wall at the end of the small room. As if guarding the bed, there hung a black and white oil painting with various lines and geometric shapes and the whole piece had to measure four-, or five-feet square. It was some sort of interpretation of what unquestionably had to be S.'s worst nightmares, expressed through the medium of modern art. I found it rather Picasso-esque, minus the disembodied eyes and misplaced breasts, of course.

The heels of my white canvas Keds [16] were still touching the stained wooden doorway threshold when I felt J.S.'s body heat close-in on me, pressing me, moving me, pushing me, *committing* me to that bedroom! What the heck was happening? Where were L. and the other girls? What on earth were the guys downstairs thinking? What was going on? I truly had no earthly idea.

Nevertheless, panic washed over me as I tried to focus my thoughts on how to get myself out of there. I nervously stammered,

"*OK, um, let's go back downstairs ...*

Don't you think we should go down?

Let's get those Cokes and go back to the rec-room...

I've seen enough art for now, let's go back...

Don't you think L. should be here by now?

Maybe I should just wait outside."

Other than a few grunts, J.S. became silent as a grave. Momentarily, though I could hear my own voice and my soul seemed to somehow be dissociating and separating from my body, as if allowing me to watch from a psychologically *safe* distance on the far side of time's veil. Nervously, I tried to giggle just to lighten the awkwardness of my situation; but I realized it only made me sound like a *silly little girl*. However, if you think about it, after all I <u>was</u> just a *silly little girl*! Ahhhh! I felt so small and seemed to definitely be shrinking infinitesimally smaller by the nanosecond — hopefully into an invisible wisp so I might just float away — far, far away.

To my knowledge and recollection, I had never gotten myself into a sticky situation and sort-of backed into a corner, as it were, without being able to joke, flirt or talk my way out of it. But my wit and my words were useless and not working for me this time. As he pushed me with his body I yelled,

"NO J.!! NO! Stop! Stop it!

What are you doing?

My gosh! Why don't you just leave me alone?!

Stop-it J.! I mean it. This isn't funny.

What do you want? What do you want with me?

What the heck are you doing?

Stop it! You're hurting my hands. You're hurting me!

Why are you doing this to me? You have your own girlfriend! Why are you messing with me?"

What *J.S. knew*, and I didn't, was that *his fiancée* was **with** L. and the girls, and that *none of them* would be returning to S.'s house that day! My life really did flash before my eyes, as this huge man grabbed my small hands with his VERY large, football-throwing-and-catching *bear-paws*! Then, pulling my arms up high over my head, he grabbed both my wrists with one hand. Though my back was still to him, I *heard* him reach around behind his back and turn the locking button on the bedroom door.

Demonstrating his dexterity, with one-hand, J.S. pulled off my little pink, eyelet-lace-trimmed peasant blouse, exposing my white cotton "A" cup, Playtex Cross-Your-Heart bra [17], which came off next. (He enjoyed demonstrating his prowess at unsnapping bra hooks, one-handed.) Then he yanked down my pink and white cotton gingham, flounced mini-skort and for just a second he sort-of stared at my *little girl*, plain white cotton, lace-trimmed panties. Then, while I was squirming to get away, with vigorous delight he grinned as he pulled them off too, ripping a section of the lace trim from the right leg.

There hadn't been very much clothing to remove, and it certainly wasn't difficult for this man. He remained calm, confident, in control of me, yet in enough of a rush that my running shoes stayed on during my entire ordeal. I recall thinking that *he's done this before*. J.S. kept my wrists clasped in one hand and his other hand over my mouth as he dragged me, caveman-style, from the doorway to the bed. Unceremoniously, he threw me down onto the low, legless twin mattress and box-spring. All this occurred while I was trying to protest, fight back and scream for help through his sweaty, slimy, greasy palm! Of course it was too little, too late; he already had me right where he wanted me.

Frankly I thought he had completely lost his mind. I never saw myself as an object of lust. I could not have understood at the time, that the *rape* to which I was about to be forced to succumb, was a vicious act of control and anger, and had nothing to do with his *lust* for me. Nor was I aware at the time that rape was a criminal act, which was not simply a minor misdemeanor, deserving of only a *slap on the wrist*, but a serious felony, meriting long-term imprisonment! How could I know? The word wasn't even in my vocabulary, so I hardly knew its *meaning* or *significance*.

To me, J.S. was already an ominous individual and so strong and overpowering. I'm certain he could recognize the terror screaming from my innocent eyes. [He really didn't have to go so far as to threaten my life, or *my parents'* lives, if I ever told anyone what he'd done to me ...] I understood I was in very serious trouble, yet all I could do was to implore him to stop, and not to hurt me. But he paid no attention to my begging, my protestations or my objections punctuated by my attempted kicks. As the music from downstairs grew louder and louder, J.S. quickly set about his mission of molesting and brutally, violently, viciously raping me. While a houseful of people audibly witnessed my struggling, I could only wonder if they were all waiting, with bated breath no less, to hear J.S. relate the salacious details of his conquest, after he was *finished* with *me*. (Yet, where, I wondered, were S.'s parents during my ordeal — asleep? — away?)

Chapter 17: The Set-up

My mind tripped back to what could have been L.'s role in the "set-up" of my brutal rape? After that day I was too afraid to ask her about J.S. and the other guys, or to mention my having been raped, in case she hadn't already heard from the rumour mill which, no doubt by then, was working overtime! I simply *had* to believe she didn't know what was going to happen to me when she called to ask me to meet her at S.'s place on that fateful day. Surely, if J.S., or any of the guys, put her up to calling me, they must have told her they were going to play some little gag or trick on me. Certainly she would have had no idea I would be viciously raped and robbed of my apparently *coveted* virginity, very soon after I got to the house. I had to believe that, hopefully, she did not purposely set me up! Or maybe she was never even there. Maybe J.S. just got her to phone me from wherever she was at. Maybe she was over at his fiancée's place. I could only ever ponder these thoughts and forever wonder. *I certainly didn't dare ask anyone and bring further unwanted attention to myself.*

I wouldn't know for weeks to come that there had been some ridiculous **bet** between my *then* "boyfriend", "Sticks" (E.), and his older brother R. I found out that "Sticks" had bragged to R. about "popping my cherry", boasting that he was actually the *first* man to have sex with me! Presumably in their testosterone-fueled, pea-brained world, breaking a girl's virginal hymen was deserving of such accolades! I was mystified by such abysmal idiocy — and as a matter of fact, *I still am*.

Of course, it had been a blatant lie! But, R., determined to prove his *kid* brother to be a liar, apparently planned to set me up so that *he could,* they *could all,* know the truth. (I don't really blame R. as he wasn't the one who actually, physically raped me; however, J.S. didn't really have to act upon their insane scheme ... but *he did*). Anyway, I presumed J.S. jumped at the chance to be the hero to his jock-strap buddies! He would be the one to determine the truth, and have a good time doing it!

[With the veils of time and space separating my "now" from my "then", it has suddenly struck me that by J.S. "raping" me, it is such a dark irony as *he* was actually the first man to penetrate my sealed vagina, splice my hymen, deflower my pure and untouched body and spill my blood!]

Why in the hell would these guys even care about my virginity? I was a "nobody"! I was an insignificant little girl. I was private and kept to myself. I was secretive, and *had thirteen years of good reasons for being so!!!* [But that is a whole 'nuther part of my story.] I got along with everyone and in fact it had been said about me that I "could make friends in an empty room"! Why me!? I couldn't imagine it was just to reveal that "Sticks" was a liar and in doing so, make fun of *him*! But why was this crime perpetrated at my expense? I couldn't believe anyone could concoct such a condemnable scheme.

I suppose it goes without saying that I figured "Sticks" discovered the plan and knew about my rape, so I stopped seeing him immediately. I never told. I never reported J.S. out of fear of retaliation. He went free and never paid for his crime of *STATUTORY RAPE* of **me**. In fact, he still walks freely and lives freely to this day. I often wonder how many times he repeated his violent raping of young "innocents" — virgin, or otherwise!

Unfortunately, in 1964 there were NO "RAPE Crisis Centres", NO "RAPE Counselors", or NO hospital "RAPE Evidence Kits" to preserve possible physical fluids as proof of who committed the rape in order to proceed with criminal charges. "DNA" had long since been discovered, however its usefulness in forensic identification for genetic profiling would not even be discovered for another twenty years [18]. If a woman cried "RAPE" it was always turned back on her. In fact, women were actually warned by the authorities that if they are being, or have just been, *raped* they should shout "**FIRE**!!" as this would bring a positive response, and someone would be more likely to rush in and help! The real consensus of opinions would be that,

"The girl/woman must have done something to warrant or deserve it." or,

"It couldn't be nearly as bad as she is trying to make everyone believe." or,

"She must have led the boy on, worn slutty clothes, enticed him or acted like some kind of whore!

or, "She must have already **had** a bad reputation."

The girl was virtually *always* blamed and interrogated until there was nothing left of her own "self". She would try to defend, beg and plead, but no one would ever believe her, *ever*! No, it was no use, no use at all in 1964, never any use to request such help from the Man/the Law! In any event, I certainly couldn't *tell anyone* because the scandalous report would, upon reaching my poor Daddy, send him completely into a deadly tailspin, since he was already on the verge of losing his battle with death's bony grasp. My Daddy spent many months over my five years of high school, (the same period prior to his death), admitted into Toronto's Sunnybrook Hospital intensive care units. He suffered greatly with repeated, dreaded, Congestive Heart Failure, choking Emphysema, excruciating Angina, and the terrifying Narcolepsy which was undiagnosed at *that* time.

I knew Daddy kept a pistol in the bottom, left drawer of the antique, mahogany desk in his study. He had always told me "BUNNY, IF ANYONE EVER HURTS YOU IN ANY WAY, I WOULD KILL THEM WITHOUT HESITATION!" Daddy knew he didn't have much longer to live and, with nothing left to lose, would have gladly taken lethal action against J.S. and of course any, and all, of the others involved in the vile scheme. I'm sure he would also have "punished" those responsible for *not* stepping-up to help me. However, one terrible crime against our family had already been perpetrated and having my Daddy murder my rapist would be two crimes too many. I knew my Daddy would never survive such a horror.

No, I determined that my poor, pitiful, frail Daddy could never, never, NEVER know! So, the question facing me at that point was, "*What now*?" I asked my soul if my life was worth anything. What if anyone looked in my eyes and discovered the secret behind the charred and blackened depression now beginning to creep across and poison my brain? My soul's answer would be a resounding, "**NO! My life is garbage; it's filth; it's crap**!" With full knowledge of this fact, I had to face the reality that *everyone* in the entire high school *knew* what should have been only *my private secret*!

During the course of the school years to follow, (which were the entire first year, and four more to follow, since I was in the five-year Arts & Sciences program in the Ontario Grade 13 curriculum), as I was forced to walk past the senior boys' lockers en route to the cafeteria, eventually I even *lost my dignity*. I spent every school day until I graduated grade thirteen, walking those halls, just trying to hold my head up. Realizing that *they* <u>all</u> *knew* and sensing them jeer and laugh at me, was almost enough to make me stop eating in the cafeteria all together.

So, in order for my personal emotional survival, my secret motto eventually became,

"Fake it until you make it."

Chapter 18: "MONSTER"!

I waited fourteen years — **fourteen years**, until I was twenty-eight. Within the depths of my soul, I had sequestered my secret and kept silent for almost ten years after Heaven's rapturous wings encompassed my Daddy's tormented, pain-wracked body, easing his soul through time's gossamer veil, to be enveloped in the loving arms of his waiting Lord and Creator. I was only nineteen, when my Daddy had to *leave* me — forever — just nineteen, when all the pixels of my universe crumbled to miniscule uncollectible bits which imploded, scattering past infinity.

Fourteen years of holding my secret close to my heart abruptly ended with an opportunity which manifested in such a way that there was nothing else to do, but to tell "Mother" of my long repressed anguish and pain — to disclose *my secret*. In fact, if circumstances hadn't presented themselves at that time, I believe I would have waited *forever*.

Unbeknownst to my gentle, loving, saintly Daddy, my adoptive, so-called "Mother", had been a controlling, abusive, battering, molesting **Monster** to *me,* for all thirteen years of *my life* prior to my rape. Daddy had *no idea* about her treatment of me, because she always acted syrupy, sickly sweet to me *in front of him,* or, for that matter, *in front of anybody else* — especially the neighbours or the *church* people. Publicly, she'd kiss me and hug me and repeat how much she loved me. However, it was an *act* which managed to convince Daddy that any rift between us was *my doing.* He would repeatedly direct me to, "*Be good to your 'Mother'.*" or "*Do whatever your 'Mother' tells you to do, no matter what.*" When she regularly complained to him that I had been very "wicked", or "talked back" and deserved a "lickin'", [which was always untrue as my life with her was, for me, a matter of minute-by-minute of walking barefoot on eggshells], she would insist *he* spank me, but not tell him she had already done just that, only with her chosen implements of torture! Daddy would seem so helpless and pathetic, because he knew he couldn't argue with her or undermine her authority. Inevitably, however, he would take me to my room and quietly explain, "*Sweetheart, you know I always tell you that you should obey your 'Mother' and do whatever she tells you, without questioning her.*" He would say, *"Bunny, you know I don't want to spank you but your 'Mother' insists you deserve this* punishment. I want you to know that this is going to hurt me more than it hurts you — and someday I hope you will understand why I'm saying this."

Then he would put me over his knee and with an open palm, lightly spank my bottom, (though never bare), two or three times at the most. I didn't cry until I looked into my Daddy's eyes and saw *him* crying. I didn't cry from the pain or indignity of the *spanking*, I cried from the anguish and torment emanating through my Daddy's eyes, from his damaged heart's depths. That's what hurt me far more than any of the abuse *she* perpetrated on me ever could. Daddy was so loathe to administer a spanking that I can say I received such punishment from him fewer times than the fingers on one hand.

Contrary to my Daddy's difficulty in administering even the smallest amount of physical punishment, "Mother" had daily been *physically beating, emotionally* and *psychologically battering* and *sexually abusing* and *molesting* me, ever since my earliest memories,* after my adoption at six weeks of age. "Mother" would repeatedly holler about what a **bad** little girl I was. She'd scream and accuse me of being "wicked" and "evil" and I needed to have the "bad little girl *beaten out of [me]*"! She regularly insisted I belonged "in the gutter with [my] 'mother'". She'd call *me* my "mother's" "cast-offs" like some tattered old hand-me-down shoes that even my alleged *gutter-dwelling "mother"* had no use for and tossed in the trash. "Mother" often reminded me she wanted nothing to do with me. She refused to accompany Daddy when he first went to get me and in fact, when he first brought me *home*, this woman's unmotherly attitude began with her immediate refusal to *ever* change my diapers. Daddy had to change me in the morning, travel home by bus on his lunch hour to clean me up and change my diaper, and then repeat the chore after work and throughout the night. He had to bathe me at night, prove there were no monsters under my bed or in my closet, then read me bedtime stories and sit with me and sing or hum until I fell asleep. Daddy took me to the Saturday library story-times and puppet shows. He even arranged for me to ride in the little red, green and gold coloured "Santa's Elf Train," so I wouldn't have to march all along the route in the freezing cold snow and ice, at the Toronto Santa Claus Parades.

*[This includes both my earliest "recalled" memories, and my memories elicited from counselling sessions, hypnotherapy and psychotherapeutic hypnotic age regression sessions.]

"Mother" was ashamed of me and would regularly agree with her friends who said she and Daddy were just "too old" to be my parents. The fact that I had blonde hair and blue eyes, while theirs were brown and brown, didn't do anything to endear me to her. "Mother" often told me she sincerely wished I were **dead** and that when my Daddy brought me home to be "theirs", it totally ruined their lives. She said, "Your father and I would have travelled around the world and had a wonderful life, instead of being saddled with an unwanted cast-off — you!"

"Mother" controlled every aspect of my existence, *except* for my loving relationship with my Daddy — (she couldn't touch that!) She even used *food* to torment me. One night during supper, I told her I hated lima beans, and the next day when I came home from primary school for lunch, she forced me to eat an entire can of those slimy green things. Later, back at school I vomited the entire mess of half-digested lima beans all over my classroom floor! (Naturally, a note was sent home informing my parents of my unexplained "illness".) On another occasion I was on my way home for lunch, again from primary school, and I had to step over a little birdie's fresh guts that were strewn across the width of cracked sidewalk in front of me. Of course I was upset to see the dead little bird, but worse, my stomach was doing flips from seeing the stringy, red intestines. When I got home and was crying about the "dead birdie", I told the *Monster* exactly what I had seen. What did she force me to eat for lunch? She opened a small *can of spaghetti in tomato sauce* and poured it out, unheated, onto my plate! It looked exactly like the birdie's tangle of bloody guts! "You sit there and you eat that, right now!" she demanded. I was whimpering, "But it looks like the birdies insides. I can't eat it, please don't *force* me to." But the steel-edged wooden ruler, which clipped my temple just above my right ear, perpetrated the *forcing*, and I had to eat the *whole* can with her sitting and watching my every bite. Back at school, I raised my hand to ask to go to the washroom because my tummy felt sick, but my teacher didn't believe me. Once again I hurled the entire can of undigested, barely chewed spaghetti noodles all over the classroom floor! This time my vomitus triggered the same reaction in *two* other kids, and you can just imagine what the classroom looked, and smelled like at that point.

Sadly the teacher again sent a note home to notify my parents that there was something *wrong* with me. What did the Monster do? She hit my head with one of her very favourite torturous implements — the yardstick, and so many blows I lost count and I "fell asleep". [I was actually rendered unconscious.] I knew it really hurt where she hit my head and ears, but I didn't know I had blood oozing from my right ear until Daddy came home. When he started washing my hair in the bathtub before bed, he noticed something sticky and dried into a thick, hard lump in my hair.

"Mary, what's this lump in your hair?"

What happened Bunny, dear?

Did you fall down, sweetheart?

How did you hurt your ear, baby?"

"Kay dear, come in here and look at Mary's head. It's been bleeding somehow!" Daddy urged.

"I just sat down — you bring her here to me!" the Monster whined.

She explained that she had no idea what happened and went on ad nauseam about, "Oh, poor dear!" But when Daddy turned away to get my nighttime glass of milk from the fridge, she scowled at me and mouthed the words: "Don't you tell!" Of course, I didn't dare breathe a word of what she had done, for fear of further repercussions from her. There were many secrets like this one that I was forced to conceal all my life — until now, until <u>this very moment</u>.**

[**Of course, my secrets *were* divulged to my counsellors and therapists over the decades of my therapies.]

This Monster constantly succeeded in making me feel very small and helpless, and definitely useless and *stupid*. I could do *nothing right* in her eyes, and equally, *nothing wrong* in my Daddy's eyes. These feelings were exacerbated in situations such as the time my elementary school Principal sent a letter to my "parents" which read,

Dear Mr. and Mrs. MacDonald,

After considerable testing, we have determined that Mary is already successfully working well above the fourth grade level. We are very pleased to inform you that Mary is one of our choice of only three students who are more than qualified to skip grade five and, beginning in the fall term, she will start the six grade. Please sign your acknowledgment of this notice on the appropriate lines and return it with Mary at your earliest convenience. Thank you and congratulations. Yours truly ...

I was supposed to "skip" grade five and jump right from fourth to sixth. WOW! I was so excited and really felt validated that perhaps I was a little "smarter" than the Monster had always led me to believe. However, although Daddy strongly disagreed, the Monster said I wasn't bright enough, or capable of handling the course work. She insisted I shouldn't do it and she refused to sign the school's directive. I felt completely deflated, disappointed and betrayed, and even more so when my best girlfriend, Anne, *was allowed* to skip ahead. Sadly, eventually *this* would prove to be a situation which took a noticeable toll on our friendship as Anne moved on, making new, older friends in the sixth grade, leaving me bored and treading water, behind her in fifth.

****

I had always been such a good little girl. I sang in the church and school choirs and I studied violin for seven years and practiced for two hours every morning before school, and even on Saturdays. Daddy loved it! — I hated it. I just did it for him, and for him I achieved awards, medals and money for my performances. I played "principle second violin" as a member of the school orchestra and we performed at venues such as the O'Keefe Centre in Toronto. I even soloed in a recital at Carnegie Hall in New York City. I did it all to please my Daddy because of his immense, unconditional love for me. Due to his *bad heart*, he and I both deeply understood, [and often discussed], our time together on this earth would come to an end far too soon. I only wanted to do anything just to please him. I also played French horn and flute in the school orchestra, but I had asthma and didn't like the flute, and the Horn was almost as big as I was; far too big for a little gal like me to tote back and forth to school. Of course, this left my dream of learning the piano, which I *really* wanted to do, and dragging one home from school every day, totally out of the question. So, violin was the only logical choice of instrument, and always Daddy's favourite anyway.

Chapter 19: Rulers, Yardsticks and Other Torturous Implements!

It is still excruciatingly painful for me to disclose *all* of the details of the molestation and torture I suffered at the "Monster's" hands. Suffice to say that she used utensils and implements such as: rulers, yardsticks, hair brushes and wooden spoons with which to beat, batter, poke, jab and molest me. The origins of any marks the implements left on visible areas of my skin were dismissed as my roughhousing with friends. When "mother" used a wooden school ruler, the kind with the hard, sharp metal strip all the way down one edge, cleverly, she would be certain to only use it on the bottoms of my bare feet, (which looked as if caused by barefoot outdoor play), or on my head, ears or neck, because my long curly hair would usually disguise the cuts it made.

I couldn't cry. If I cried, she'd hit me more and more, and even harder. I learned to ABSOLUTELY NEVER cry in front of the Monster, no matter what! I would hide and sob alone in the cellar, amongst the spider webs behind the monstrous, noisy, scary old coal furnace, or in the narrow space between the garage and the fence, where the weeds kissed the sky. Or, I'd weep silently into my pillow at night. I really wanted to cry to Daddy, except, imagining the Monster a "saint", he wouldn't understand my tears, and *I* certainly could never tell him the real reason.

This Monster's other favourite torture was to use the old enema bulb to even take control of my insides! It was a reddish-brown, tear-drop shaped rubber reservoir with a long, black plastic nozzle that bulged at the end. Almost daily, she would fill it with *cold* water and something like dish lotion, and she'd bend me over and ram it up into my bum. Then she'd make me sit on the toilet with that damn thing sticking out of my bum, and she wouldn't let me get off until she *"said so"*. Sometimes she'd come back in and hit me if it had fallen out. Then she'd refill the cold water and shove it back up in me, and again squeeze the bulb. The cramps it elicited were agonizingly painful. Usually, I sat there on the toilet for so long, the sharp inner edge of the wooden toilet seat created red marks indenting the back of my thighs and my bum. Often she'd go back downstairs and *forget* me! Once, I even fell asleep! There was nothing I could do to stop this horrendous "punishment". She'd threaten much worse if I ever told Daddy about her torturous game with this enema bulb. I sooooo wanted to run away. I even wanted to join-up with the circus — just a dream, though, because I couldn't run away. Somehow, innately, I understood that it would hurt my sweet Daddy and exacerbate his illnesses — maybe even kill him.

The Monster's torture of me had only ended in the spring of my thirteenth year, just a few months *before* J.S. raped me. The ending began on a Saturday morning when she had once again crawled into my bed and undone and her robe, pressing her naked torso up against my "sleeping" body. However, I was only sleeping lightly and her weighty movement on my mattress had immediately *awakened* me. I kept my eyes squeezed tightly closed and pretended to still be deeply sleeping, because I hoped and prayed she would just get up and leave me alone this morning. It wasn't gonna happen. When she started in on her ritual molestation, I *knew this time* I just *had* to think of something, and do whatever I could to stop her, once and for all time. [Of course, I think it's obvious why she always made me wear only a nightgown to bed, with no panties, and why she hid-away the handsewn pajamas my "Auntie Myrtle" annually fashioned for my Christmas presents.]

This particular instance I had been sleeping on my back when she pulled my nightie up and started fondling and kissing my budding breasts and my little nipples. I could barely stand it — *it felt awful!* It was sickening and I didn't know what to do! *I wanted to puke!* I thought I would die if I didn't hit her, or something! But, then she spread my legs apart and started manipulating my genitals with her fingers, until my body began to respond with natural lubrication. I felt like squirming away, but didn't want to reveal my awakened state. "Physically", it felt weirdly good, but I knew it was **bad** — I just didn't know how to stop her, or exactly *what* she was doing to my body, or why. I wondered what she could possibly be doing to me that could simultaneously feel awful and wonderful. My mind was on fire! What to do? How to make her stop, forever?!

Just then, when I was *wet* enough, she grabbed her tortoise-shell hairbrush, that she'd brought with her and had placed where she could easily reach it on my night stand. My muscles reflexively stiffened as I sensed she was about to beat me, but instead I felt her force its plastic handle into my wet vagina. She began repeatedly moving it in and out, masturbating me, as *she* moaned with pleasure, while masturbating her own vagina with her the fingers of her other hand. It hurt and felt, well, indescribable at the same time. All these strange feelings emanating from between my legs, and the moaning sounds that I've always thought I only dreamt about hearing, I suddenly realized were **_very real_**! And, yes, they seemed to come to me in my dreams, but now I understood the dreams, nightmares and night terrors of monsters were not dreams at all. They were *this* Monster's regularly repeated incidents of sexual molestation. There was only ever *one* Monster — and *she was very, very real*.

I have no idea where I got the emotional strength, but my anger welled up inside me and that's when I balled-up my fist and swung a very hard punch right in this so-called "mother's" direction. My eyes were still shut, so I only guessed if my fist would connect with her head. But, I got her right in the eye! She was dumbfounded and started screaming at me and slapping my face to "wake me up", complaining that I had just punched her. She was crying and re-buttoning her pink terrycloth housecoat, and going on and on about how I was "very wicked" and that I was "really gonna get it now!" Then, as I tried to sit up, I realized I still had the hairbrush sticking out of me, between my legs. When she saw me looking at *her* hairbrush, she started screeching that I was "soooooo bad" and acted "just like [my] mother — that wicked slutty whore!" *** "What are you trying to do with *my* hairbrush between your legs? And why did you punch me in the eye, you wicked little guttersnipe?" Fortunately, my fist had happened to seriously blacken her eye pretty quickly.

***[She had never met my birth "mother" Berneice Ketteringham Faulconer, and knew absolutely nothing about the woman who was not only **not** *a slutty whore*, but in fact was also married to my father, when she was lured, deceived and had me literally ripped away from her loving arms — breaking her heart and mine, forever.]

I was naïve and truly couldn't comprehend what she was trying to do to me rolling my nightie up around my neck and then sticking her hairbrush inside me, or why she was naked and had been pressing up against me on the bed. I had no idea what to say, or ask. How could I understand she was using my young body for her personal perverse orgasmic pleasure? How could I verbalize that this true-life *wicked witch's* secret, depraved, clandestine activities, gave her some sick form of sexual gratification. All I did know was that it felt very icky, creepy and wrong, in a moral sense. However, even more confusing was the fact that *physically*, my body responded the way any young girl's would naturally respond to sexual stimulation — with pleasure approaching orgasm. This was a very confusing mixed mental message, that something so obviously evil being perpetrated on me by the "Monster", could actually, physically feel so delightful. All I could do was to *act as if it didn't happen.* Nevertheless, I did muster enough gumption to ask her,

"What were you doing to me?"

"Never mind whatever your dirty, wicked little mind *imagines* you think I was doing with you! Just you look what you did to me, you spoiled brat! Ohhhhh! What were you doing sticking my nice hairbrush into yourself? You must do this all the time! Do you? Yes, of course, you dirty little girl! You must stick things inside of you all the time! Why are you doing this wicked thing?" Then she leaned to look at her face in my dresser mirror and screeched, "Look what you've done to my eye! I was just leaning down to give you a little 'Good-morning!' kiss, and you punched me so hard! Now I have a black eye, and tomorrow is *church* day! What am I going to tell everyone? You are going to get the beating of your life when you get downstairs!"

At that point she grabbed the brush, still sticking out of my vagina, and before she pulled it out, she rammed it in — hard, which really hurt me a lot — but I didn't dare cry. I couldn't understand what she was doing, or why. What could I do? What could I say? At that point, despite her disgusting actions, I was confused and at a loss for words, and all that would dribble out of my mouth was,

"Oh, I'm so sorry, mom, I was dreaming I was playing baseball and just hit a home run!"

I had hit that home run all right! — I had punched her eye when I caught her in the act of *molesting me* for what, thank God, became the <u>very last time</u>!!!

She knew that *I knew* she was doing this awful thing to my body and that it was not only disgusting, but also very, very inappropriate and wrong for anyone to do to someone else, let alone their child, and even worse, their own *adopted* child who really *belonged* to another "mother"!

****

[If you are reading this with any skepticism and find it difficult to comprehend how a woman, a "mother" or an adoptive "mother", could "molest" a baby, a toddler, a child, a 'tween or a teen girl entrusted to her so-called "loving" care, consider the novel, and true story of, "Sybil" [22]. I had always assumed this type of perverse sexual manipulation, assault, and masturbatory "rape" was a common occurrence between ALL little girls and their mothers — adoptive or natural. However it wasn't until I stumbled upon the 1976 movie, "Sybil", based on the book of the same name, that I began to experience the sliver of the possibility that my "Mother's" behavior was abnormal, perverted and just plain sick! I watched that television movie with great uneasiness and difficulty. Yet, I couldn't bring myself to turn it off and by the time it ended, upon recognizing the similar abuses and torture that Sybil's natural "mother" perpetrated on her as a little child, Sybil's story became a vindication for me. I finally began to see that what this evil Monster was doing to me, *did* actually *happen*, and was not only *very, very wrong*, but also a criminal act. This perpetrator was the woman I always treated as my "Mother", even though she *never* treated me like her "daughter".

But of course, with the exception of my therapists who were sterile, clinical, formal, restrained and necessarily "non-judgmental", I could never reveal my dark truths to anyone — any *real* people, until right now as, I am finally relating this to you, my reader. This has been most difficult, embarrassing and excruciatingly painful to face, admit to and write about. However, after many years of psychotherapy including: group therapy, Gestalt, and Cognitive Behavioural Therapy as well as meditation and prayer, I am expressing exactly that which I had always loathed the very thought of escaping from my mind, and either off my lips, or into any manuscript. For the sake of exposing the ugly truths in my life I have walked with courageous steps to face, and expose, my own darkest demons.]

****

"Mother" and I never again discussed the "black-eye" incident, or her fetish for using me for mutual masturbation. She would never know, just as I wouldn't know for decades to come, that the perverse actions she committed against my body and soul would have long-term, and far-reaching consequences for my future emotional, sexual and mental health. Her abuse convinced me that any form of sexual intimacy is a very wicked thing. I couldn't justify or accept the overwhelming physical feelings when her perverted actions brought me to the confusion of orgasmic pleasure. From her I learned that, worse than the action itself, the natural response of a girl's/woman's body while being sexually stimulated in one way or another, either by a man or a woman, or inanimate object, is a very, very, **very bad** thing!

The actions by this MONSTER in fake "mother's" clothing succeeded in tainting the budding delights of my first "true" love, of all my life's experiences of loving intimacy and even the natural intimate maternal joys of nursing my children. This Monster's sexual abuse set me up for a future of failed relationships and marriages. I believed I was damned to hell for being part of her little "games", even if I was usually asleep, and/or too young and naïve to comprehend that she was sexually gratifying her own self by "raping" me with implements. For me, the guilt was overwhelming.

The only "mother" I ever knew taught me an important lesson that would colour my life until this very day. I learned that there is only one value to my life, and that is in acknowledging that any, and all, hate-filled abuse, torture, beatings and molestations as being the only way I could be accepted by others. It was the manner through which I understood I could be "loved" by anyone in my life. My misguided understanding of my body, who owns it, what it should be used for, and how it should always be abused, taught me *to spread my legs for acceptance and love*. I understood the only way to avoid a beating, was through offering sex. Throughout my life, the more sexually creative I became, the more I was accepted by individuals — by men. I have been married four times, (five if you count dating and living with P. for five years), and each marriage was driven by my eager, originative, abundant, ceaseless sexual "appetite". (God help me if I ever had a *real* headache.) No matter what I felt or desired personally, my most vital duty in my marriages was to first, foremost and always, sexually delight my husbands. This was in no way, living the life for which I was destined by my Creator. Nor was this validating, or even remotely creatively reinforcing for my soul.

My only hope for escaping my mistaken and misdirected understanding of who I am, or was ever meant to be, and what value I have to offer to the world, has been through the finality of divorce and my eventual chosen celibacy. Only then — only now, am I able to express the poetic lyrics of my heart as I probe the depths of my soul to understand my personal value within this universe.

Chapter 20: Ahhhhhhhhhhhhhhhhhhhhhhhhhhhhhhhhh!!!!!!!!!!!

The Monster was always complaining about being "in pain", and remained unhappy, morose and generally quite miserable. Until she was ninety-two, she continually whined that she thought she was *dying*. She complained about everything and nothing. Finally, one afternoon, I was driving her to the local K-mart and she was going on and on, bitching ...

"*You have no idea about what it's like to live in pain!*"

"*You never had anything go wrong in your life!*"

"*You live such a charmed and perfect life!*"

"*You never have any problems!*"

"*BLAH! BLAH!! BLAH!!!*"

[Was she serious!? How about the fact that I was ripped from my birth "mother's loving arms at the age of six weeks? What about the fact that I was brought home by my loving "Daddy", and handed to **her** to share in my daily care while Daddy was at work, completely naïve and unaware of her true attitude and actions toward me? What about this witch telling me she wished I had "never been born" — or this psychotic molester saying she wished I were "dead, and already in the ground" — and flat-out telling me so on many occasions?!]

That was it! I just couldn't hold it in any longer! I exploded, fairly vomiting the words I'd been restraining for fourteen years —

"*God Damn you — you complaining bitch! I sure have had problems — VERY, VERY serious and devastating problems, and they all started with YOU, and YOU KNOW IT! In fact, there is something that I never told you or Daddy about. I tried to spare you both the pain of knowing what really happened to me. At the tender age of fourteen, I WAS RAPED! VIOLENTLY, HUMILIATINGLY RAPED and STRIPPED of MY SELF-WORTH, MY DIGNITY, MY JOY, MY INNOCENCE, MY TRUST and MY LIFE!!!*"

"*Raped?*" she hummed, then added,

"Raped? Are you sure?" **[Was I sure??!!]** *Then she* **hissed**,

"Maybe you were just ASKING for it! I'll bet YOU WERE, weren't you!?? So, tell me, what were you wearing?"

No doubt, witnessing the abhorrent shock on my face, all she could next say was,

"Well, that's too bad."

I was sobbing uncontrollably when, as an after-thought she added,

"Well I'm in pain too, so **let's just forget it and say it never happened***. Take me into the store now, I want to do my shopping!"*

Ahhhhhhhhhhhhhhhhhhhhhhhhhhhhhhhhhhhhhhhhhh!!!!!!!!!!

[Again my pain-wracked soul silently screaming]

Nineteen years later in 1997, thankfully, as I stared down at her cold, wrinkled, pasty white, formaldehyde-plumped flesh, I realized she was finally going to be out of my life, forever. In all nineteen years after disclosing my rape by J.S., it was never mentioned between us again. Of course, her thirteen-year abuse and sexual molestation of me was *never* mentioned between us. But, even as she approached death, only *her* pain was the issue, and *not mine* — never, ever, ever, ever mine …

However, I finally did get the last word on this MONSTER. She had insisted on an open casket so all her family and friends could whine about what a "terrible loss" her demise had caused them to suffer. She'd hope they would wail and wipe their tears and cry, "Oh…poor K. and oh, poor us for our loss…" But she didn't know in their next breath they would express their true feelings about her death, "Sure hope she left us all a bundle of dough!" [I am not exaggerating.] However, immediately prior to the mortician moving her casket to the viewing area for the funeral, I INSISTED on a closed, casket that was nailed shut! I was in charge. It was only me. I could finally do what I wanted with this witch, and I did! I nailed her in that pink, satin-lined mahogany casket, forever!

"Ahhhhhhhhhhhhhhhhhhhhhhhhhhhhhhhhhhhhhhhhhhhhhhhhhhhhhhhhhhhh!!!!!"

[The sound of relief; of a breath; of *my pure* breath, inhaled and exhaled in complete and final freedom.]

Chapter 21: Wiser Eyes: Removing the Rose Tints

As I rewrite this for the final time I have just seen sixty-five come and go. All five decades of my life following my rape have been filled with my thoughts of every imaginable means of retaliation, of avenging my innocence and my life, irretrievably broken forever. I have dreamed of tracking down J.S., *somewhere* in Toronto, I imagined, and torturing him with the biggest butcher knife I could lay my hands on. I planned on gouging his bulging, pasty-white belly in huge, deep circles — in the same way he gouged me. I wanted to *core* his ugly, wrinkled penis and his testicles and shove the bloodied, slaughterhouse mess into his mouth, so he, himself, could enjoy the delights of this member that he mistakenly seemed to think every woman so desperately desired!

Ahhh, yesssss! Then I would watch his body bleed-out from the gaping hole where his "manhood" *used to be* — as he slowly, very, very slowly died. Then I envisioned myself laughing, cackling hysterically at him while he suffers humiliating physical, mental and emotional agony. Then, repeating his words right after raping me, I'd shout,

"Haaaa! So, *you were a man!*"

I have repeatedly thought of this plan, dreamed of these actions and prayed for such revenge one day. Of course, however, these are only the imaginings and rantings of one of J.S.'s rape victims whose psyche has been devastated from his violent assault and the fifty-one years of secret emotional pain which followed.

Chapter 22: "...never tried this before!"

Now the events of my life have taken me from 1964 when I was raped, to 1969 when I graduated L.H.S. and left Toronto for the University of Guelph, then McMaster University, subsequently graduating both by 1973. Seven years later, I moved to Tennessee, then Mississippi, (graduating from two other universities), back to Tennessee and up to British Columbia, Canada. Overall, my relocations have taken me 6000 miles in the span of thirty-seven years and never once did I cross paths with J.S. At the time of publication, it is 2015 and fifty-one years after my rape in Toronto and I still live in the Canadian province of British Columbia. Purposefully, I am as far west across Canada as I could possible live from Toronto, and from the memories of my youthful rape.

Several years ago I clicked on an internet pop-up for Classmates.com, an online classmates' reunion site. Though I had never done such a thing before, I thought it time I reconnect with some old friends from high school. Surely they would have forgotten, or forgiven, or have mellowed attitudes over the years. I had to believe it would be OK *now*. So I did connect, and signed up, putting my name out there in case any old L. High Schoolers (L.H.S.ers) were on the same site. Though I was hesitant and a little fearful of being *discovered, peeled, revealed* and *devastated* again, I figured I was physically so far removed from Toronto that it would be safe enough to just enter my *general* location as *B.C.* only, not disclosing my city.

At that time, the first of only two people to contact me on that site was B., a self-appointed, one-man force with a determined mission to reunite old L.H.S.ers. It felt good to have a sense of reconnection through B., since, I was pretty certain, (from the welcoming tone of his email), he must have been one of the few who *did not know* about my "past".

But then, almost immediately after B., the _second person_ to contact me on that site was **J.S.!** *J.S.!* *Forty years* after raping me, this man wrote a short email on July 23, 2004 at 2:45 pm which read:

> "*Welcome to BC, Mary* I was glad to hear that life is good & wish you well. J.S."

Ironically the subject line had read only: *"never tried this before!"* That was *it*! That was the whole message! I could hardly believe my eyes. Of all the possible people who could have seen my name newly listed on the site and sent me a welcoming email, what were the chances of it being him? Did he *really* not know who I was? Could he have forgotten what he had *done to me* forty years earlier? Did he think himself clever for writing to ME? *Why* did he write to *me* — especially if this was the first time and he'd, "never tried this before"?

In fact, I believed that J.S. *did* know who I was, and what he'd done to me, and he decided to write me perhaps to see what I might say, or if I remembered it was *him*. He was "text-book"; truly a classic narcissistic, socio-pathological personality, (as I have come to understand such abnormal psychological behaviour).

I started thinking about J.S.'s greeting: "*Welcome to BC Mary*". Deciphering that he was likely already living in British Columbia, Canada, was not exactly rocket science. Now this is a very big province, with many, very large cities within the borders of its 945,000 square kilometres. The city in which I was living, was on Vancouver Island and was a good sized city on a very, very large island surrounded by the Pacific Ocean. Strangely enough though, I started feeling most uncomfortable, having been one of this man's *victims*. In my mind, I had a "flash forward", believing I could be facing the future possibility of always having to "look over my shoulder" in fear.

Although I hardly expected to find any information, nonetheless out of discomfort and curiosity I looked for J's surname, "S." in my relatively small city's skinny little phone directory. I was only wondering: "What would be the chances?" When I landed on the listing under, "S-------", there it was, attacking me again from the directory pages, larger than life itself: J.S.'s street address and phone number! I had to read it over repeatedly until it sank in that he lived only a few blocks away — walking distance, literally right down the street from me! My brain ached with the unfathomable statistical possibility of the chances of this happening by accident. (Or perhaps it was not an accident that *I* ended up *living there*.)

I sat in total shock, numb with thoughts tumbling over themselves, all racing toward some degree of hopeful clarity. All the years of hate and plans for revenge lined themselves up in front of my brain like the pattern of black and white keys on a piano. It was yes and no, over and over, and over, and over. It became quite clear what I *had* to do. The "yes" and "no" manifested in black and white, (with a little touch of *red* splashed in). I could end this nightmare forever, quickly, neatly. Who would know? Who could possibly know? Who ever knew?

The old thoughts and plans began erupting through my consciousness. I made the decision to, once and for all time, gouge the life blood from J.S.'s body, just as I could still sense the moment he had symbolically done to mine. It felt good to me to be so close to achieving that which I had spent decades in quiet musings, clouded daydreams and darkened nightmares *accomplishing*.

Wanting to ascertain that it was really J.S., I tried repeatedly to phone the number, ready to hang up quickly if *he* picked up the receiver. Finally, unbelievably I got his answering machine with what I recognized, even after all the years, to be J.S.'s voice. He had recorded a teasingly smart-ass message, saying the number belonged to himself and his "*partner*"! Of course, I hung-up without speaking. I recall thinking he didn't want anyone to know if he was married, single or just "shacking up" — no doubt, as always, wanting to keep his options open!

Within minutes, I couldn't control the tsunamic urge rushing forward within me, so I drove over to J.S.'s apartment building. I sat in my car outside the small, weathered, old white building that rose only a few storeys. Pensively, I waited and watched until time lost all significance.

I never got out of my car.

I never saw J.S.

And ... I never went back.

Chapter 23: Forgiveness?

Very slowly something began to worm its way into my altered mind-state. I began grasping at whatever knowledge I had gleaned from two of my degree majors: Psychology and Philosophy, combined with the experience of several of my recent years' of heavy involvement in a "Bible-thumpin'-fire-and-brimstone-preachin'", Southern Baptist Church down in Mississippi. All of this knowledge and these experiences slowly began to ease me in the direction of considering the concept of "forgiveness".

I had learned about, and tried to practice this principle which requires a person to be completely *forgiving* of someone who has been deeply and intentionally hurtful to them. I tried to accept that at some level of one's psyche, releasing the resultant anger or hatred for, and pardoning of, someone who has deliberately wronged you, can be very cathartic, even healing. (Naturally, "forgiveness" is not meant to condone a person's violent actions, it only permits the forgiving of the *"human being"* who perpetrated such viciousness.)

Could releasing my hatred for J.S. heal me of decades of mental anguish and resulting physical pain? I wondered. I was certain I could never forgive his brutal actions. Nevertheless, in trying to forgive the man, if not the act, I was supposed to feel a cleansing ocean's wave of peace washing over me and erasing the past's dark undertows.

Suddenly, after never having taken a deep breath in forty years, my chest moved up, my ribs broke open and, as my lungs deliberately and slowly expanded, purging air rushed in. I held this air, this deep, deep breath, as if it were my most precious possession. I never wanted to release this air from my lungs, never.

Nonetheless, as one inevitably must do after inhaling, I *exhaled*. Through this cyclic, promised exchange, I began receiving an energy I had not experienced in forty years. It had begun in my heart, rushed across my chest and down both arms. My hands and fingers took on a new strength, a heat, a power. I stood up from my desk and felt the warm rush of energy radiate down both legs. (Much different, I mused, than the memory of that old *trickle of blood* ...)

Breath, release, strength, energy, power, empowerment — I did not consciously understand the process. However, on a guttural level, I totally and completely knew that the "victimization" within me had been pushed slightly aside by this overwhelming, endowing energy. I wanted it to be over, all over, completely over! *I* was the risen Phoenix — the survivor and the winner.

With these new thoughts in mind, bravely, though admittedly nervously and somewhat facetiously, I emailed J.S. back on that site later that day.

[In my defense, I was attempting to appear nonchalant, casual, and virtually hopeful of somehow *inviting* a dialogue with J.S. I was almost thinking that he just might slip-up and say something in reference to his having raped me forty years previous to his "Classmates" email to me. I thought if I could keep some line of communication open and *light*, he may just get cocky and sound-off to me or, hopefully, say something incriminating. Additionally, I wanted him to know that I KNEW that we not only lived in the same city in British Columbia, but only blocks apart. ... And, ultimately of course, I wanted and deserved J.'s confession, and perhaps even an apology! But, just in case ... I also wanted to keep open my option of torturous murder.]

On July 23, 2004, at 9:39 p.m., my reply email to J.S. read as follows:

"Subject: *RE: never tried this before!*

You know what, J.? I would not have been more surprised to watch a squirrel whistle 'O Canada' than I was to hear from you!!!!!!!!!!!!!!! I appreciate your good wishes, and right back at ya. Some sweltering weather we're having here *in [this city] today, isn't it? Mary*

PS I'd never tried this before, either."

****

J.S. never replied to my facetious email response to him. And sometime thereafter, he moved 513 miles away to Prince George, in inland British Columbia. He went so far as to begin self-identifying by using his middle name of "S------". "S.S." then took a job working as a coach and University lecturer in Marketing. One could only assume that he made these changes to his name, location and career in order to *not* be easily found by any of the victims he *thought* he'd left behind years before in Ontario — and God only knows where else!

****

[I have to add here something that has been on my mind since I first heard about it several years ago. I am speaking about the "Highway of Tears" [23]. This refers to Highway 16 in mainland British Columbia which runs right through Prince George. This particular highway is infamous for the outstanding number of "missing and murdered young women" who were last known to be walking or hitchhiking along its route. No one has ever discovered who has been abducting, raping and/or murdering these women who are mostly indigenous, and to date number approximately forty-three. My concern is, "Did anyone ever think to question J.S, or "S.S.", who was living and working in Prince George?" This man is a known rapist, not only of myself, but also likely of at least one, or both, of the "twins" at L.H.S., and no doubt many others over the years in the two, or more, provinces. I know he was capable of serious violence, even beyond criminal rape, as, certainly in my case, he made no bones about threatening my life and the lives of my family members. Of course this is only a *thought* in my own mind and I have not, as yet, approached the RCMP with my question.]

Chapter 24: Disclosing My Secret

Just a few months after J.S.'s strange and shocking email to me, B. decided to arrange a mini class reunion in my city on Vancouver Island. In an attempt to coordinate a meet-up, he contacted the handful of L.H.S. alumni who ended up living out this way and would be close enough to get together for a few hours. Needless to say, J.S., with full knowledge that I, not only RSVP'd that I would be attending the mini-reunion, but also that he and I in fact lived only a few streets apart, offered a flimsy excuse and declined to attend.

****

Indeed, as arranged, I did meet with B. and his wife. It was a grey day and the weather was chilly with a light rain, befitting my apprehensive mood. When I arrived at the Denny's Restaurant I discovered that, unfortunately, no other graduates living out this way were able to attend our little reunion. Nonetheless it was fun to meet with B. and his wife. After a couple hours of mindless chatter, updates and memories, my mind began to drift. I listened politely, nodding in agreement, while B. repeatedly lamented the absence of those three or four other L.H.S. graduates unable to attend our little reunion.

From his continued reminiscing about the *good ol' times*, with all the football and hockey jocks, I understood that B. was especially disappointed that his good buddy, J.S., could not meet us in the Denny's that day. B. knew, as did I, that "J-bo" was actually living *just up the street*, not even a five-minute drive away from the restaurant! His excuse was that he had to be out of town for one reason or another. Nonetheless, B. was visibly disappointed.

So as not to reveal my secret, I kept silent, swallowing my painful memories that were being dredged up. However, I could bear the emotional anguish only until it re-manifested physically as that familiar old pain in my abdomen, just below my sternum. Oh God, it was that damn ulcer — my silent, ever-present, pre-strike warning system! Oh hell, there it was rising up my chest and into my throat. I bit my lower lip in a futile attempt to block the pain, took another gulp of my *milk* and pushed it back down into my gut! But then, I began to feel the tension of that dreaded, and sadly familiar, "steel band" tightening around my skull.

Though I tried to concentrate on B.'s and his wife's faces, their words began piercing me like a hundred daggers. I couldn't fathom how they continued focusing on, and glorifying J.S., this asshole—this thief—this violator—this rapist—this criminal—THIS FELON!

Momentarily, B.'s words started to garble and the lights of the restaurant appeared to be flashing in those terrifyingly familiar strobing patterns. I knew the electrical storms had begun striking all over the surface of my brain. It was the rumbling storm-front of another horrific migraine, of course. Immediately, I knew our visit would have to be cut even shorter as *I* couldn't stay much longer.

Realizing this would most likely be the very last time I would be seeing B., I knew it was possibly my final opportunity to tell *my story* — from *my perspective* and face-to-face so they could see I was not fabricating any part! Repeatedly the questions raced through my mind, tormenting me silently and secretly.

Should I tell?

Dare I tell?

Would they even believe me?

Would it matter?

How would it change anything?

Did B. already know?

What did he know?

Who else knew?

What should I say?

Could I ever be forgiven?

I decided to feel him out to determine once and for all *if* he really knew — and *what* he actually knew, because if *anyone* knew, it would be B. He always had his finger on the pulse of the

L.H.S. goings-on. I believed *he* always had intimate knowledge of the "who's-who", and "what's-what" on, or off, our high school campus. And if B. *knew* — I was convinced that the entire school *had known*, and this had always been my greatest fear driving one of my worst nightmares.

At a lull in the conversation I looked right into B.'s eyes. My mind, having conveniently *dissociated* from my body, (a regular occurrence in such stressful situations), permitted me to '*watch*' from a safe distance as the words vomited out of my mouth, spewing across the table's distance, and letter-by-letter, *bouncing into* their ears,

> "*You know I am quite relieved that J.S., especially J.S., was unable or, more likely unwilling to meet with us. However, I am not surprised that such a **coward** could not show his face* to me *in person!*"

Hearing my words, B. looked at me in *beyond stunned* silence. Nevertheless, I continued,

> "*Personally*", I told them, "*I have not been looking forward to seeing J.S. face-to-face either. I didn't know, and actually I was afraid of, what I may say to him.*"

I swallowed deeply, took a long, slow breath and with more courage than I have ever had, spoke these words to B. and his wife,

> "*You see, J.S. **raped** me when I was innocent, naïve and just a child, having only **just** turned fourteen ... and yes, of course, I was also a* virgin*!*"

Although B. and his wife seemed genuinely astonished at my accusation, neither said much other than the expected, flimsy condolences, somewhat along the line of, "Oh My God, Mary ... what you must have gone through!"... with other such condescending, though seemingly genuine, expressions.

Continuing, I clasped my hands tightly together in my lap in an attempt to disguise my trembling, then I related a brief synopsis of my story. Quite surprisingly, B. did *not* appear terribly judgmental. His wife's only reaction was a straight face, blank except for a few sorrowful nods, which considering the graphic nature of my accusation, I thought really quite odd.

Then I told them I had always been certain the entire school had known and that it would have been common public knowledge that J.S. had raped me. I explained that I was also positive I had been painted as the harlot who *seduced* the *innocent* foot-baller! Of that much I was beyond certain, due to the sudden parade of older "boys" trying to *date* me, and EXPECTING to have sex with me following my rape!**** And because of *my* newly acquired "bad reputation" after the rape, I found myself in a position of never knowing whom to trust — surely not any of the girls now, and even more certainly — not any of the boys, no matter whomever I *thought* I *knew* before the incident!

B. and his wife stammered mutual denials of any knowledge. He weakly tried to reassure me that I was *not* the centre of the rumour machine and that, to his knowledge, nobody, with the obvious exception of those in the house at the time, no one else ever knew! I nodded again, but my mind was racing as my disbelief of B.'s saccharine words overcame my ulcer pain and the ever-tightening band of metal around my head.

As the time neared for them to be heading out to catch their ferry, we started saying our polite "Good-byes". Just then, with some hesitation, B. decided to disclose something he believed to be true which was both shocking and validating for me. He said, "You know, Mary, I've always been curious and wondered about 'the twins'". He exchanged a quick glance with his wife whose face was still an emotionless blank wall. Then he continued to explain that there were rumours, from quite *legitimate* sources, that either one, or possibly both, of those pretty, popular, *virginal* twin girls at our school had also been brutally raped and right around the same year, 1964, as far as he recollected.

B. actually named the girls, however it didn't trigger a memory, as my brain was on fire with nerve impulses from my migraine. In any case, the twin's (or twins'), parents, upon discovering it was a "jock" at L.H.S. who was responsible, pulled them both out of our school, and sequestered them securely in another high school. B. speculated they were possibly even moved to a costly private school because of the shame and stigma of the rape! However, I'm guessing it was far more likely because they wanted to protect the other twin from experiencing the same fate, in the event she had not already been victimized.

****

****Incidentally, this *parade* of horny slobs thinking they could take advantage of me also included the school's sports' coach who naturally happened to be attached at the hip to his favourite *athlete*, J.S. The incident occurred when I was working on the school's yearbook, and for my article I had to go to this man's office to elicit the details about a photo of a particular sports incident. Naturally, I stood in front of his desk to discuss it with him, but he insisted I come around and examine something more closely *in the photo*. I recall I was wearing a black-and-white, herringbone patterned, knit mini-dress and immediately, when I stood next to him, quickly he put his hand up under my dress and started to finger me! I gasped and jerked away, absolutely stunned, but he just laughed. *He laughed!*

What the hell!!?? To me, this gym teacher/coach was "old, ugly and creepy". I was not on any sports teams, (unless you count the trampoline), and we had never spoken so I had no inkling what made him suddenly think he do this to me. Immediately however, I realized that J.S. had no doubt told him that, now that my "cherry" had been "popped", I'd be an *easy lay*! Naturally, nobody else was around W.'s office and instantly I realized it would be his word against mine! No doubt, he knew I had not reported my rape by J.S. and he could be fairly certain I would not say a word about his revolting and disgustingly inappropriate actions. And he would have been correct. I never told anyone and this was just one more incident of molestation which would end up being one more secret I would have to keep sequestered in my soul in order to protect *my Daddy*. And, this was only the beginning of *many* incidents with older "guys" at my high school making concerted efforts to sexually molest me after news of my rape spread around the school like wildfire!

****

Incidents of sexual abuse did not end when I left high school. One night, in my third year at the University of Guelph, I was at my "Ethics" professor, Dr. Terrance W.'s year-end "wine and cheese get-together" at his apartment. Dr. "Terry" was a greying, middle aged man who was short and slight of build. As in all my philosophy courses, I had been working at an A-to-A+ level and was regularly called-upon to assist students struggling to achieve a C. I had never attended any sort-of gathering at a prof's home, so this invitation felt quite special to me. Dr. Terry set out a vast selection of fancy cheeses which I could tell he'd had catered from the little signs giving the name of each cheese. Fortunately for me, ginger ale was also offered, because I never drank alcohol. After a lot of schmoozing with fellow students and a couple other professors, the party was winding down and as was always the case due to my asthma, the smokers drove *me* out to the balcony to get some air, before I had to bike home. The sliding glass balcony door was curtained on the inside and I was only out there for about fifteen minutes. However, when I came back in, I was shocked to see that *everyone* had suddenly, and quite surreptitiously, left and *I* was the only remaining "guest".

As I was thanking my professor/host for the invitation, he insisted I have *more* wine; but I had not had anything alcoholic to drink and politely declined his offer. I grabbed my purse and sweater and proceeded to leave when he abruptly stopped me at the door by using a key to deadbolt it. He started to press me with his body, pushing me back in order to commit me to his bedroom. I asked him to quit; in fact I pleaded with him to stop. But he ignored me and was working hard to pull my slacks and panties off when I kneed him in the groin. Then, knowing I couldn't get out the door, I ran to the balcony and started screaming, "Rape!!!!" He came out and dragged me back into the apartment and unlocked the door, pushing me out into the apartment hallway. He warned that I'd better, "*say nothing about this, because nobody would believe me anyway*", and that he was, "**at liberty to fail me!**"

I would never have told anyone about the embarrassing assault; however, my two roommates were awake when I got home. When they saw how I was trembling and the emotional state I was in, they insisted on escorting me the following morning to the campus police to report this creep's actions. I told the police *exactly* what occurred and what Dr. Terry…… had obviously planned, by secretly "ending the party" while I was out on the balcony. Sadly, the two male officers asked me,

"Are you interested in this professor?", and

"Why did you go to the party alone?", and

"Why didn't you leave when everyone else did?", and

"What were you wearing?", and

"Were you high — or drunk?", and

"Were you just trying to sleep with him to score a higher grade?" and

"Did you imagine this whole incident?"

Needless to say, the investigation of Professor Terry…… was halted, right then and there. And this "Ethics" professor gave me a very low failing grade on my final exam. I went to his office to speak privately with him and asked how he determined my grade. All he had to say was, if I had only "cooperated" the night of his party, I would have that "A+" I was expecting, instead of the "F" he was "forced" to give me! Since philosophy is a very subjective discipline, grading my exam essay was completely at this man's liberty and there was no arguing with him as he, alone, was obviously in charge of my grade. However when this "F" was added to my unchangeable previously stellar grades throughout the semester, I graduated, barely squeaking through with a pass, which was by far the lowest grade I had/have ever received in any university course.

****

Is it any wonder that for the past fourteen years that I've lived back in Canada, I have refused to "date", no matter how genuinely: "nice", "kind", "caring" or "loving" a man may appear? Though I'm now middle-aged, I often *still* have men attempting to engage me online in intimate/sexual conversations and wanting me to disclose where I live. If there has been any way to have some level of control over my body and avoid others' abuse of it, I've decided that if I don't ever allow myself to be alone with a man, I will be able to control such sociopaths and psychopaths lying in wait to again assault, abuse, molest or rape me — or worse.]

Chapter 25: Never Just Once!!

Since parting ways with B. and his wife, neither of them has ever communicated with me regarding my rape "allegation". That tidbit of innuendo, rumour or truth, regarding the alleged rape of another young girl, or girls by a "jock" at L.H.S., would have been very elucidating to me back in 1964, or during any of the painful years which have followed. I know it could have alleviated some, or maybe all of the unwarranted guilt I have continued to live with by having always assumed that J.S.'s criminal actions were a one-time event and somehow *my own fault*. Surely it would have lightened my lonely burden of trying to carry that secret, its stigma and my shame for these five decades! Perhaps I would have learned and understood that the responsibility for the rape was solely and totally J.S.'s, (with at least some share in the guilt belonging to S., R. and any of the other "boys" who may have *encouraged* J.S. to be the one to perform the deed). Nonetheless, my physical rape was J.S.'s fault — and only J.S.'s fault! And it would have furthered my own healing to understand that it should have been J.S., NOT ME, who should be the one bending and weakening from the weight of the decades of guilt associated with HIS having raped ME, so many years previously!

Nevertheless, something was still nagging at my mind as I was looking back from that reasonably safe psychological distance. I understood at that moment, my 20/20 hindsight had been crystalized by a matured and well-educated mind. I was ultimately aware that the probability of J.S. perpetrating other rapes, and/or molestations of children/girls from our school, or even in or around the Toronto suburb of L., would be extremely high.

I have actually come to learn over these pain-riddled decades that the child molesters, the child sexual abusers and the child rapists NEVER, EVER, EVER commit their heinous acts only once! It is absolutely never an isolated incident! Their established routines and patterns for procurement and grooming of those of us "innocents", and the repetitive methods they utilize to violate us, are perpetuated for their own pathetic and cowardly self-gratification, whether driven by their sexual perversions or aberrant need to control young girls! Their crimes usually go unpunished for years, decades ... even lifetimes ... at least until after the second or third incident of being caught in the act. Of course, sometimes they are never held accountable for their vicious felonies.

Wistfully, I wondered what if ALL of J.S.'s possible rape, molestation and abuse victims were brave enough to band together? Surely we could expose him for the heinous and monstrous perpetrator he was and possibly, no, *probably* still is! But how would we, or could we, ever have justice, retribution or renewal of our precious selves? The flowers of our innocence which he most violently and viciously ripped out by the roots, could never again sprout new blooms — absolutely never!

Over fifty years, yes, FIFTY YEARS, is the length of time I have kept this secret locked away inside my heart. I had pushed all of my horrific memories down very deeply into my soul's "lockbox" and behind its ever-vigilant gatekeeper, burying them in the deepest recesses of my wounded heart. However, throughout my life when these dark, traumatic memories slipped past the gatekeeper into my conscious awareness, I shook my head and silently screamed "NOOOOOOO!!!!!" My mind would race and *run* from the resulting fear and torment. And on more than a few occasions *I* literally, physically ran. Yes, I actually ran in hopes of ridding my mind of its torment!

This trauma inflicted upon me in my very young life succeeded in halting my natural maturation process, essentially freezing my emotional development at the age of fourteen — forever! My innocence was fragmented for what has seemed to be an eternity, and my inability to *trust* has succeeded in haunting me and ruining virtually ALL of the relationships that followed in my life — either with men, or women.

I pondered a sad anti-climax to my reunion with B. and his wife. It was the realization that J.S.'s victims' collective innocence was then, and would be until forever, as irretrievably vapourized as a distant star, long dead by the time we first glimpse its light. In place of innocence would be a bottomless, unending black hole. And this *non-space* of negative existence having raped the innocence from our lives, would leave in place only the permanent, empty expanse of our imploding, collective, ***innocence presumed***.

I know that some secrets are best kept forever; but, not this one, not now, certainly not ever again — and not for me.

Chapter 26: Letter to J.S.

To: J.S. who raped me, S. who attempted to rape me, R. who was in on the heinous plot, and all the other men in S.'s house that day, who neither prevented, nor stepped in to stop, J.S. from RAPING me.

This autobiographical novel, my memoir, has presented a true account of how J.S.'s actions, (or the others' inactions), in 1964 ruined my life and, no doubt, the lives of countless other victims of abuse, molestation, torture, rape, and God Himself only knows what else.

I am not writing my heartfelt memories in order to empower you or give you any further control over my life. However, J.S., being the true, dyed-in-the-wool narcissistic sociopath that you have demonstrated yourself to be, I'm certain you *will* feel exactly that way.

I write these once-secret memories with only one intention in mind — to elicit the truth! I want the truth to be known about myself, and if upon my disclosure of these details, the truth about any others victimized by you wish to tell their own truths, I will add theirs to mine and re-publish this memoir to include details of their true accounts as well. This is not a threat, but a vow!

The truth J.S.!

Right now, J.S., I have only one thing left to say to you, and it is this:

At this present moment you are on the downhill slide of middle age, speeding toward the great finale of your miserable life — your final "touchdown", so to speak, and that will be your death! You are, at the time of publication, approximately, 68-69 years of age. I have seen your photograph and you are balding, paunchy and your once toned and tanned "footballer" physique has no doubt turned to grotesque, flabby, white, dimpled, cellulite-covered blubber! Envisioning you like this is **my** retributive justice. I have determined that you do not need to suffer actual physical demise at the hands of either myself, or any of those of us who have been your innocent victims. From here on until your death, you would do well to take to heart the words of Robert Deniro's character, from his famous movie "The Deer Hunter": **"No Means No!"** [17]

Chapter 27: The Vicious Cycle

The greatest and most devastating irony of my horrendous childhood experience of rape, was not so much the fact that it ruined *my* life, but that it fueled my hope to never bear a daughter, for fear that one day she might, herself, become a rape victim. I have been pregnant eleven times in my life and miscarried ten babies. Finally, at thirty-four I did bear a beautiful, perfect son; but then God in His Infinite Wisdom saw fit to indeed grace my life and *entrust* me with a precious baby girl when I was thirty-six. Though I always feared for her safety from any horrors such as I had experienced at the hands of J.S., I tried to put such fears out of my mind and raise her with abundant love and as much security as I could provide. As she approached thirteen, I considered telling her about my experience, yet I feared she might judge me, or worse, not believe me and would become too naïve and trusting of all men. I *never* knew when, if ever, the time would be right to tell her about my own rape, or when she would be mature enough to comprehend it and stay alert and aware of such possibilities in her own life.

At what age can you protect your children, girls or boys, with what you have learned in life, but without shocking or traumatizing them? A rhetorical question, yes, but because of the world we find ourselves in these days, it's a vitally important one. Unfortunately for me, the answer to this question came far sooner than I would have imagined. Without ever having *the talk* with my daughter about my own rape, and without my knowledge for a full year after occurrence of the incident, my beautiful, sweet, happy, bubbly, innocent thirteen-year-old daughter was in fact *brutally raped* by a neighbour, in the middle of the day! He was the husband in the family for whom she was doing a little "supervised" babysitting, (since she was only two doors down from our home in our little cul-de-sac, in Horn Lake, Mississippi). I never knew anything about it. She hid this dark, horrific secret because she didn't feel safe disclosing it to me, knowing how her violent, abusive, controlling step-father would likely turn it all around and blame and punish her.

On Thanksgiving Day, as I set the "turkey with all the trimmings" on the table, and we were just about to sit down to dinner, the phone rang. It was our neighbour, the "mother" of the two- and four-year-old little girls that my daughter occasionally babysat. The frantic woman told us that she had just discovered that her husband, Cody, had not only been raping their own four-year-old daughter, but was also bragging about raping *my* daughter the year before. Worse still, he admitted to friends that he was planning to *rape my daughter again* "as soon as [he] could get the chance", and he had in fact been stalking her for this very purpose! He also indicated he was thinking about next raping his own two-year-old daughter.

We confronted my daughter who admitted Cody had indeed forcibly raped her and she gave details of the other people who were in the next room and could verify her version of events. Of course Cody's wife had already notified the police and we immediately involved the police and the court system as well. This man had laughingly bragged to several witnesses about his crime of statutory rape of, in the very least, two little girls — his own daughter and mine as well. The justice system moved unusually swiftly in this case and Cody was found "guilty" of statutory rape of my daughter and, at the age of twenty-three, was sentenced to a term "no less than thirty and no more than forty years". He was incarcerated in Mississippi State Prison which is better known in the mid-south U.S.A. as, "Parchman" [21], the state's oldest, most notorious, and only maximum security prison for men, and one which also had a separate "death row" [18].

It was too late to protect my little girl from this cowardly excuse for a man, but not too late to see retributive justice for her, because her rapist was a small, blonde-haired, Caucasian man in a prison in which 98 percent of inmates were large, muscular, African American men who were convicted hardcore rapists and murderers. I believe Cody sealed his own fate and his karma in Parchman would no doubt be immediate, swift, violent and *repeated* rape for all of his years of incarceration! For my daughter's rape this was as satisfying a result of closure as we could hope for, or expect, since *execution* was off the table.

However, of course, for myself it is too late to even hope for any justice for J.S.'s criminal rape of me, so, for his culpability, his continues to be, "**presumed innocence**". And, for myself, unfortunately I must accept that there will *never* be any satisfactory closure — **never**.

Chapter 28: And the Beat Goes On…

At the time of publication, I have a beautiful, bright, healthy, precocious seven-almost-eight-year-old granddaughter — my daughter's little girl. All that my daughter and I can only hope and pray for this child is that this repetitive, cyclic nightmare of rape has ended with my daughter and such a violent crime will never be perpetrated on my little granddaughter. We both know we will eventually have to enlighten her as to the horrors that men can commit — the only question is, "When?" — At fourteen? That was too late for me! — At thirteen? That was too late for my daughter! — At twelve?! Oh my God, when *can* an innocent little girl possibly understand *rape*? When? And why should she have to be educated about, and forced to understand, such horrific possibilities for her own life?

Appendix "A"

Something rarely discussed are all the deleterious effects of childhood sexual molestation and rape on the victim later in life. A few of my own symptoms, mentioned herein, have been: blinding migraines, anxiety and depression. But the psychopathology in later life is far more complicated and extensive. Personally, I have experienced, and/or been diagnosed with, the following: paralyzing anxiety, debilitating depression, low self-esteem, victimization, self-inflicted harm, (five suicide attempts), inability to form trusting relationships, difficulty with intimacy, secrecy, Accommodation Syndrome, chronic low back pain, helplessness and conflict in interpersonal relationships, (four failed marriages), mental breakdown, panic attacks, Dissociative Disorder, Post-Traumatic Stress Disorder (P.T.S.D.), Fibromyalgia, and Bipolar I Affective Disorder.

I am not alone as a victim/survivor suffering such physical, mental and emotional issues. According to Martin & Fleming (1998),

> "… the fundamental damage inflicted by child sexual abuse is due to the child's developing capacities for trust, intimacy, agency and sexuality, and that many of the mental health problems of adult life associated with histories of child sexual abuse are second-order effects." [24]

****

"I always call sexual abuse in childhood the gift that keeps on giving, because it can be a single event but it can affect a lifetime."

Drew Pinsky, M.D. [26]

Epilogue

I have experienced life-long psychological, emotional and physical repercussions from a childhood of abuse, rape, molestation and battery. My issues began with my original victimization by my adoptive "mother" and were cemented with my rape by J.S. Yet, regardless of a background which I understand would have devastated many for life, I have been able to somehow rise above my personal darkness and apply myself in my educational and career endeavours in order to achieve a measure of success. Now that I have finally disclosed my life-long, painful secrets I am releasing them from my heart so I may now focus on the *other* stories in my life. Of course, if I am approached to help another soul express their memories as memoirs, my mind, now free of its own darkest shadows, will also be free to help others illuminate and accept their own.

In the words spoken by the elderly "Rose Dawson", in the James Cameron film, "Titanic" [20]:

"A woman's heart is a deep ocean of secrets."

But, for this heart, J.S., my ocean's secret, "**is**" no longer.

References

[1] Roosevelt, Eleanor. Moncur, Michael. (2013). Roosevelt: Eleanor Roosevelt. (1884-1962). *The Quotations Page.* Retrieved from, http://www.quotationspage.com/search.php3?homesearch=roosevelt&page=10

[2] von Kleist, Dave. Writer, broadcaster. Retrieved from, http://davevonkleist.me/

[3] Angelou, Maya. *Brainy Quote.* Retrieved from, http://www.brainyquote.com/quotes/authors/m/maya_angelou.html

[4] *"Beach Party"*. American film. Retrieved from, https://en.wikipedia.org/wiki/Beach_party_film

[5] *Frankie Avalon and Annette Funicello.* Retrieved from, https://ca.images.search.yahoo.com/search/images;_ylt=AwrSbl2flaNVyB0ArpfrFAx.;_ylu=X3oDMTE0c3M1cHFtBGNvbG8DZ3ExBHBvcwMxBHZ0aWQDVklQQ0ExMV8xBHNlYwNzYw--?p=Frankie+and+Annette&fr=crmas

[6] *Bobbittize.* Retrieved from, http://neologisms.rice.edu/index.php?a=term&d=1&t=5071

[7] *"Molson's Canadian"* beer. Molson's Brewery. Retrieved from, https://en.wikipedia.org/wiki/Molson_Brewery

[8] *Percale sheets.* Retrieved from, https://en.wikipedia.org/wiki/Percale

[9] *Coke.* Registered Trademark of Coca-Cola Beverage Company. Retrieved from, https://en.wikipedia.org/wiki/Coca-Cola

[10] *Cover Girl Cosmetics.* Retrieved from, http://www.covergirl.com/

[11] Mogen David wine. *Wikipedia.* Wikimedia Foundation Inc. Retrieved from, http://en.wikipedia.org/wiki/Mogen_David

[12] *Revlon Red lipstick.* Revlon Home Products. Retrieved from, http://www.revlon.co.uk/Revlon-Home/Products/Lips/Lipcolor/Revlon-Super-Lustrous-Lipstick.aspx

[13] *Welches' Grape Jelly.* "Drinking Glass" collectibles. Retrieved from, http://www.ebay.com/itm/Vintage-1960s-Hanna-Barbera-Flintstones-Welchs-Jelly-Glasses-Embossed-Bottom-/121698487231?pt=LH_DefaultDomain_0&hash=item1c55cb8bbf

[14] *GHB gamma-Hydroxybutyric acid/gamma-Hydroxybutyrate.* Retrieved from, http://www.drugabuse.gov/publications/drugfacts/club-drugs-ghb-ketamine-rohypnol

[15] *"Mr. Clean".* Proctor and Gamble cleaning products. Retrieved from, http://www.mrclean.com/en_US

[16] *Keds Shoes.* Retrieved from, http://www.keds.com/en/home

[17] *Playtex Cross-Your-Heart Bra.* Playtex brand ladies' undergarments. Wikipedia. Wikimedia Foundation, Inc. Retrieved from, https://en.wikipedia.org/wiki/Playtex

[18] DNA. *Deoxyribonucleic Acid.* Wikipedia. Wikimedia Foundation Inc. Retrieved from, http://en.wikipedia.org/wiki/DNA

[19] *The Deer Hunter.* (1978) American film directed by Michael Cimino. Wikipedia. Wikimedia Foundation, Inc. Retrieved from, https://en.wikipedia.org/wiki/The_Deer_Hunter

[20] *"Titanic".* (1997) American film directed by James Cameron. Retrieved from, https://en.wikipedia.org/wiki/Titanic_(1997_film)

[21] *"Parchman Prison".* Mississippi State Penitentiary. Retrieved from, http://en.wikipedia.org/wiki/Mississippi_State_Penitentiary

[22] Shrieber, Flora-Rheta. *Sybil.* (1973). Independent Publishing Group. BookRags online. Retrieved from, http://www.bookrags.com/studyguide-sybil-flora-rheta-schreiber/chapanal001.html#gsc.tab=0

[23] Kameir, R. (2014). *Canada's Highway of Tears and the women we forgot.* GAWKER 5/21/14. Retrieved from, http://gawker.com/canadas-highway-of-tears-and-the-women-we-forgot-1579002464

[24] Fleming, J., Mullen, P.E., Sibthorpe, B., Bammer, G., (Feb. 1999). The long-term impact of childhood sexual abuse in Australian women. *Child Abuse & Neglect* 23(2): 145-59. PubMed. PMID: 10075184. Retrieved from, http://www.ncbi.nlm.nih.gov/pubmed/10075184

[25] Kentler, K.S., Bulik, C.M., Silberg, J., Hettema, J.M., Myers, J., Prescott, C.A. (Oct. 2000). Childhood sexual abuse and adult psychiatric and substance use disorders in women: an epidemiological and co-twin control analysis. *JAMA Psychiatry. Archives of General Psychiatry* 57(10): 953-9. Retrieved from, http://archpsyc.jamanetwork.com/article.aspx?articleid=481660. doi:10.1001/archpsyc.57.10.953

[26] Pinsky, Drew. (2015) From, "Dr. Drew" show on HLNtv which aired on 8/19/2015 21:00:00. Retrieved from Cable News Network A Time Warner Company. Retrieved from, http://edition.cnn.com/TRANSCRIPTS/1508/19/ddhln.01.html

About the Author

In her forty-year formal career, Ms. Ketteringham began as a Marketing Researcher, Proofreader, Copywriter and Editorial Assistant. Later she became a Reporter, Journalist, Feature Writer, Assistant Editor and Photographer for a USA newspaper. She has also been a University Job Analyst, Researcher and Job Description Writer; a K-through-12th grade English, Creative Arts and Science Instructor; a University Journalism, Creative Writing and French Tutor; a University Audiovisual Services Manager, Media Coordinator and Languages Department multi-language Laboratory Tutor. Presently, she is sole contributing Author, Editor and CEO of both MEMORIES to MEMOIRS PUBLISHING and PARAGON ECLECTIC EDITING. She has authored the autobiographical novel ,"Revolving Doors: The True Account of the Full Spectrum of Fostering Abuses of a Boy Before Age Five", (LULU.com), which is her brother's true story of being forced through seventeen foster homes in which he suffered unimaginable abuse, battery, molestation, torture and, yes, *rape,* before he turned five. As well, she has authored and edited several magazine features, short stories, essays and poems. She is currently a candidate for the degree Doctor of Philosophy in Metaphysical Parapsychology and holds a Bachelor of Arts, Majors: Philosophy, Psychology and English, Minor: Art; a Master of Arts in Education, Major: Childhood Creative Arts; an Associate Diploma, Majors: Journalism and French; a Diploma, Major: Early Childhood Special Education; and an Ontario Grade 13 Diploma, Major: Five-year Arts and Sciences. She considers her most meaningful titles to be: Mom, "Gam Gam", Sister and Friend.

www.ingramcontent.com/pod-product-compliance
Lightning Source LLC
Chambersburg PA
CBHW032050090426
42744CB00004B/145